FALCON

Marryat

PRINCE OF FLY FISHERS

Marryat

PRINCE OF FLY FISHERS

The life and times of
George Selwyn Marryat

TERRY LAWTON

ELLESMERE
MEDLAR PRESS
2010

Published by The Medlar Press Limited,
The Grange, Ellesmere, Shropshire SY12 9DE
www.medlarpress.com

ISBN 978-1-899600-48-9

*The Marryat flies for the colour plates were tied by
Richard Slaughter and photographed by Andrew Herd.*

The chapter opening drawings are from Halford's Dry-Fly Fishing in Theory and
Practice. *Drawn by Moul from photographs taken by Elliott and Fry.*

Extracts from the Flyfishers' Journal *appear with
kind permission of the Flyfishers' Club.*

*The author and publisher would like to thank all those who
have given permission for copyright material to be reproduced
in this book. If any have been inadvertently overlooked they
will be pleased to make the necessary arrangements.*

Designed and typeset in 12 on 13 point Garamond Roman.
Produced in England by The Medlar Press Limited, Ellesmere, England.

Contents

Dedication

*For everyone who is interested in the
history of fly fishing and
who appreciates what the
old masters can still teach us today.*

Introduction

George Selwyn Marryat's personality and ability with a fly rod made a great and lasting impact on his peers, amongst whom were the leading fly fishermen of his day. During his short life he was known as the best fly fisherman in England and then, after his death, he was referred to as the prince of fly fishers. Marryat started to make his impact on the small world of Victorian chalkstream fly fishing when he met an angler much better known today, F. M. Halford. Marryat and his place in fly-fishing history are too important to be left unrecorded.

He has always been an enigma so one of the challenges of writing this book was going to be finding information about him. But my research into his life and times - including books and magazines at Cambridge University Library, online, and at the National Archives at Kew - revealed much more information than might be imagined in some areas, and, frustratingly, much less in others. Quite a lot of his military record - seemingly lacking in any real distinction - survives but we know little of the time that he spent in Australia. Why did he go? Did he fish when he was there? He was there before the first successful shipment of brown trout ova so if he did fish it would not have been for trout. Nor would he have fished a dry fly as he did not learn how to until after his return from Australia.

We can only speculate on what might have happened to the development of fly fishing - particularly dry-fly fishing - if Halford had not met Marryat that day in Winchester. Would Halford have gone on to achieve all that he did with Marryat's influence and help? Halford certainly had much for which to thank Marryat. Marryat had far more knowledge of entomology than Halford and was adept with a microscope and an expert at mounting subjects for examination and display.

Halford encouraged Marryat to work with him, following their first meeting and initial day's fishing together. In 1929 G. E. M. Skues - best-known as the father of upstream nymph fishing - wrote what has been described as a considered assessment of F. M. Halford and his fly-fishing life. Skues had often been a harsh critic of the man and the two had had an uneasy relationship although they had fished together on the Hampshire chalkstreams. Halford had even offered to propose Skues for membership of the Flyfishers' Club in London. In his assessment, Skues wrote of the 'magnificent justification of Marryat's choice of Halford to be the prophet of the new cult' - that of the dry fly. A thought-provoking point of view and one, as far as I can identify, peculiar to Skues. It has been suggested by many that Halford could not have produced his books and fly patterns and the code of dry-fly fishing without the close collaboration, inspiration, support and friendship of George Selwyn Marryat. I cannot disagree with that proposition. But is Skues right to suggest that Marryat *chose* Halford as his prophet? It must have been serendipitous.

Another 'what might have' is what might have happened if Marryat had lived a longer life? He could have lived well into the first or even second decade of the twentieth century when he would have witnessed and probably helped the development of lighter, shorter split-cane fly rods and silk fly-lines, as well as all Halford's new dry flies. I am sure that he and Skues would have met on a river somewhere and would have been able to discuss his early attempts at tying and fishing nymphs and how he was, perhaps, discouraged from developing his ideas by the dry-fly fanaticism of Halford. I am equally sure that he would have given short shrift to those who condemned Skues and others who wanted to fish artificial nymphs to fish seen to be feeding on nymphs. Would he, perhaps, have been persuaded to join the Flyfishers' Club?

One fact that is well-known is that he had never committed any of his fishing knowledge or other experiences to print: except for two short letters, one on fly tying, the other on the history of the dry fly. Would Marryat have achieved more or written something for publication if he had not met Halford when he did? Did Marryat refuse to be named as the co-author (which he thought to be impractical) of Halford's first book because he sensed that Halford was after all the glory to be gained from the publication for himself, although Halford suggested that he had conceived his book as a joint project? Marryat undoubtedly had influence on Halford's subsequent books and this begs the question of whether he felt that, through Halford, he had said everything that he wanted to and so felt no need to write a book himself. Some have claimed that he did not have the ability to write a book but I believe that is quite incorrect. Marryat was a gifted letter writer, his uncle was the famous Victorian novelist Capt. Frank Marryat whose own offspring were also published writers, as were other members of the family. R. B. Marston, then Editor of the *Fishing Gazette*, thought that he had got him to agree to write an article on making nets which Marryat had suggested. Marston was to write: 'But he was not to be caught. No offer would tempt him to write.' If he had lived longer would he have been moved to write a book? He would not have been short of material.

Marryat was a very competent fly dresser and a patient teacher of both his fishing friends and professional fly tyers, although he seems to have stopped tying his own flies (in about 1886) in favour of buying those produced by commercial fly tyers - some of whom he helped establish and develop their businesses through his patronage. He taught Halford all that he knew about fly tying and was intimately involved in the development of the upwinged dry fly. Halford wrote: 'He was always trying new materials and new methods to make the artificial fly a better imitation of the natural insect.' After he stopped tying his own flies, he does not seem to have completely abandoned the idea of developing new patterns. At the Fisheries Exhibition of 1896, George Holland had on display examples of 'the late George Selwyn Marryat's last novelty in way of a design for Mayflies'. More flies can be attributed to him than even his contemporaries did at the time of his death. The Little Marryat - and its improved version the Quill Marryat - is his most famous legacy but there were certainly ten other patterns that he developed.

One thing that I found strange was that so few of Marryat's peers were aware of the flies that he designed and developed. Did they not see them when they fished together? His peers described him as a most unselfish fishermen who was only too eager to help and advise his fellow angler. And they must have discussed fly patterns after a day's fishing 'dinner being over, and the tobacco burning'. Red Spinner (William Senior) wrote of discussions between Marryat and Francis Francis: 'The anecdotes they could tell, the hot discussions waged over a wing or hackle or the general principle of dressing and using a fly were something to remember.'

The Little Marryat was about the only one that they knew of. But my researches threw up many more. As I gave this matter some thought (when walking my dogs), I suddenly realised that I had the benefit of being able to research Halford's books which detailed most of Marryat's designs. While Halford's first book, *Floating Flies and How to Dress Them* was published during Marryat's life - in 1886 - and then *Dry-Fly Fishing in Theory and Practice* (1889), his other works were all published after his death, in the years between 1897 and 1910.

But Halford's first book did include Marryat's Little Marryat, his Fisherman's Curse, Red Tag variant, Corkscrew, Needle Brown, Red Spinner and others. Why did his peers not know this when they wrote their heartfelt and very personal tributes to him on his death? Another little mystery to which there will never, sadly, be an answer.

Although he seems to have led a full and easy life of a well-to-do country gentleman, it was not without personal tragedy. He and his wife Lucy Dorothea's third daughter Alice Lucy, who was born in May 1877, died the following April, having suffered from inflammation of the kidneys for four days. He came from a large family with more siblings than I expected and his wife was very well connected. He lived in some interesting houses, including Mapperton House in Dorset and, from the mid-1880s, a fine house in The Close of Salisbury Cathedral with a large household of servants.

We know - from contemporary accounts and photographs - that he could handle a fly rod and out-fish any other living angler. He knew how to handle other people's rods and was able to instruct his fellow anglers, including Halford, on the finer points of casting. He also had the ability to repeat casts accurately for the camera. How would Marryat have measured-up against today's leading practitioners of the art of the fly? Anglers are given to hyperbole but if we believe only half the stories and he was alive today, fishing with his own Victorian tackle, he would at least match and possibly out-cast and out-fish many of today's very best fly fishermen. Put a modern split-cane or carbon rod and contemporary line in his hand and who knows what spectacular casting feats he would have performed. He might even have hit an individual straw in a stack!

Marryat's name lives on as the brand name of a Japanese company that manufactures fly-fishing tackle in association with a Swiss company, and with the Little Marryat trout fly - a relatively insignificant legacy for one who bestrode the banks of the English chalkstreams with such command.

When, eventually, on a very hot summer's day I stood

looking down on the simple memorial plaque in the grass of the cloister garth of Salisbury Cathedral, a strange feeling came over me. I was standing looking down on the last resting place of the mortal remains of George Selwyn Marryat, the prince of Victorian fly fishermen. Although this was not the end of my search to uncover the story of his life and times, I did feel that if I was to meet him I would have known quite a lot about him and his life.

1

The Meeting

*With the hour came the men, Mr H. S. Hall, Mr G. S. Marryat,
and Mr F. M. Halford, who evolved from the poor feeble types of dry fly
of the Seventies the efficient dry fly of the Eighties and the present day.*

G. E. M. Skues, *The Way of a Trout With a Fly*

A young, cold and probably rather bad-tempered F. M. Halford pushed open the door of John Hammond's fishing tackle emporium at the top end of The Square in Winchester at the end of a hard, cold day spent fishing the Old Barge waters of the Itchen, on the edge of the city. In spite of his best efforts he had managed to catch only two small trout. As he walked into the shop to buy some flies to re-stock his fly boxes, the jangle of the shop bell made a tall, well-built figure lounging against the counter top look up. Under the woollen tam o'shanter was the clean-shaven face of George Selwyn Marryat who was examining a number of flies on the counter top in front of him. But until they were introduced by John Hammond, neither knew the other nor to what this introduction on 28th April, 1879, was going to lead. Although the two were of very different character - Halford (often referred to as the high priest of the cult of the dry fly) was somewhat reserved and wary, and inflexible in his approach to catching trout, whereas Marryat was an intuitive craftsman who was prepared to experiment - they must have got on well at that first meeting as they agreed to fish together two days later. William Senior, angling editor of *The Field* after Francis Francis, described Halford with whom he had been 'an intimate friend of over thirty years' standing', in a book he wrote published in the 1920s:

He was thorough - thorough in his likes and dislikes, in his work, in his play, in great things, in small things, in his common sense, in the things he knew, in the things he did, in his many merits, in the clear mind that planned no less than the deft hand that executed, in the privacy of the home, and in the brazen bustle of the world of business. That is how I long looked at F. M. Halford . . .

He was a delightful companion - generous, big-hearted, amusing, a sayer of good things in a human way, and finely opinionated, which, of course, was not a serious matter when he expected and liked you to be opinionated also. He was a dangerous man to tackle in argument if your knowledge of the subject was rickety. He was emphatically what is termed a well-informed man, for that thoroughness of his stamped his knowledge, and ruled his memory. You might not always agree with him, but could seldom floor him, the ground he stood upon being rock-solid. As both a giver and taker of chaff he was an adept. He had the courage of his opinions, and none wiser than he when it was best to keep opinions an unknown quantity. In travelling or by the waterside he was wonderfully helpful if help was good for you - perhaps, if anything, too helpful, though I cannot conceive a more pardonable fault than that. Aye, Halford was verily a fine fellow.

On 30th April, Marryat was to fish the river Test with his old friend Francis Francis and Major Anthony Carlisle. Major

Carlisle was the honorary secretary of the Houghton Club which had extensive fishing rights on the river Test and was a regular contributor to *The Field* under his pen name 'South West'. Unfortunately there seems to be no contemporaneous record of the Halford-Marryat introduction nor of their first day fishing together but this is perhaps not surprising. Halford had not long been fishing the Hampshire chalkstreams and was yet to cast his dry-fly creed to expectant anglers, and Marryat was never one to seek the limelight.

The 'rubicund' John Hammond had opened his first shop in Winchester nearly thirty years earlier at the beginning of the 1850s. He took over the premises in Minster Street of his rival, H. Pottle, in 1857 and was still there in 1870 before he moved to Jewry Street in 1871, where as well as making and selling fishing tackle and flies - many of his own patterns - he was a working cutler and electro-plater. He then moved to The Square and his shop became a clearing-house for all the fishing news of the day. G. E. M. Skues, who entered Winchester College as a foundationer in September 1872, aged fourteen, was a regular visitor to his shop although it was to be two years before he could afford to buy any fly-fishing tackle. Today the shop is about a ten-minute walk from the nearest point of the Itchen by the bridge at the end of the High Street. Someone else who understood and appreciated the delights of a good fishing tackle shop was Arthur Ransome. In the opening story, 'On Tackle-shops', of his book *Rod and Line*, the first sentence that he wrote was: 'The pleasures of fishing are chiefly to be found in rivers, lakes and tackle-shops and, of the three, the last are least affected by the weather.' About halfway through the long opening paragraph, he continued: 'In the right shops is always the atmosphere of a good fishing day. Inside these shops all is confidence. All men are Selwyn Marryats and all fish are not fools, but not so clever that we shall not catch them.'

There were other Hammonds in the area, for example Hammond Brothers, gun makers, were still at number 40 Jewry Street in 1889, Miss Sarah Hammond was a gunmaker at 2 Jewry Street and next door to her, at number 1, Isaac Hammond was a gun and rifle manufacturer.

Hammond also managed the fishing rights for the Old Barge stretch of the river Itchen on the eastern side of the city. Many years later, when writing of his fifty years spent fishing the Itchen following the capture of his first Itchen brown trout on a dry fly on 20th July, 1861, Major Carlisle remembered that Hammond charged a rod fee of about £2 and that there was always a good evening rise on Old Barge. The river was so full of trout that there was never much need to move far but there were usually so many people fishing that it was all but impossible to move up and down the bank in search of a rising fish. One angler was reported to have caught four hundred brace of fish in one season. Although he must have run a successful business for many years, it was reported that when he died, Hammond left his wife and children 'badly provided for'.

Marryat and Francis Francis had been friends and had fished together for quite some years before Marryat's meeting with Frederic Halford who he then introduced to Francis. Francis was born in 1822 and so was eighteen years older than Marryat to whom he would refer in his writings as 'friend M'. Francis was a great all-round angler and thus very well qualified to be the first angling editor of *The Field*, a post he held from 1856 to 1883.

When Marryat and Halford met for the first time, Marryat was four years older than Halford. Halford had been fly fishing for only about ten years and came to the Test in 1877, aged thirty-three, with a very varied fishing background that included catching big Thames trout in the years up to 1870, and like everyone else, he was 'much impressed by his

[Marryat's] personality'. Halford had started fly fishing on the Wandle in 1868 aged twenty-four. William Senior recorded that 'In his younger days he was a great opera-goer, and never lost his fondness for music; he was an officer in the City Artillery Volunteers, and was thorough in that, and there is a silver cup that notifies his prowess at the rifle butts.'

However, on 30th April, 1879, bad weather curtailed their fishing activities so the four cold and disgruntled anglers retired to the fishing hut on the Sheepbridge beat where Marryat and Halford were soon in deep discussion about tying trout flies. A State of Rivers report - provided by 'electric telegraph' - published in *The Field* a few days later, on 3rd May, stated that the air temperature overnight at Stockbridge had been as low as 34^0 F and that there was a cold north wind. Grannom and olive duns were on the river during the afternoon and iron blue duns hatched later in the day. This was at a time when William Senior described the grannom hatch as 'an institution much regarded, and the grannom season was held in high esteem. Anglers packed their kit and hurried away when the grannom was signalled up.' And he wrote about: 'one of those marvellous rises of grannom that might be relied upon every season on the Test. Many of us who still linger have seen this phenomenon, only equalled by the hatch of the Mayfly in the Kennet Valley twenty years ago.' For many years the grannom hatch on the chalkstreams was of far greater significance than that of the mayfly. In his book *Fishing and Fishers,* J. Paul Taylor, the first Honorary Secretary of the Flyfishers' Club, included a good description of what it was like to fish on Houghton Water: 'In the Hampshire fisheries, comfort reigns supreme; and in the wettest weather (of which, indeed, we had a little) we could keep dry clothes by means of charming little huts dotted about at many a noted spot upon the banks.' During his visit Taylor stayed at Houghton Mill, where he was awakened, to his pleasant surprise, by 'the first strokes of a water-mill instead of an alarm' and he recorded that he had the pleasure of meeting Marryat one evening.

Another angler who enjoyed the experience of being woken by the sound of the water wheel and real birds was William Senior when he stayed at Houghton Mill at the end of one March. Halford knocked on his bedroom door to tell him that breakfast was ready and to advise him he was sure that there would be a hatch that day. After breakfast and on the riverbank, Senior chatted to the 'gallant "South-West" who came down[stream], and with the genial author of "the little Marryat" who came up[stream], and so got through the time all too quickly'. In further conversations Senior noted that 'M. might, at North Head, go back to his travels and squatter-ing on the Morrumbidgee' - a reference to Marryat's travels in Australia. It would seem that Marryat was not terribly forth-coming about much of his time in Australia during evenings spent yarning after a hard day's fishing as he had attended various society events and even became a provincial magistrate. Senior appreciated that he was fishing that day with exceptional anglers: 'Amongst the quartet were at least two who are fore-most amongst modern masters who have made dry-fly fishing a science, and, as everyone knows, they are its apostles. H. and M. had enough samples about them - the latter had merely come to the river-side for a stroll and chat - to last them as stock two ordinary lifetimes, yet they were full of plans for new patterns though those they had already produced were marvel-lous imitations of the duns we fished out of the water for examination.'

Halford was already forming his ideas on flies and dry-fly fish-ing that were to lead to the strict codification of the dry fly and dry-fly fishing but he was hampered in his endeavours by his lack of fly-tying ability. Quite soon after their first meeting,

Halford told Marryat of his 'difficulties in fly dressing, and he at once volunteered to give me all the assistance he could'. Halford admitted in the preface to his first book, *Floating Flies and How To Dress Them*, that Marryat had taught him everything he knew about tying flies and dyeing, selecting and preparing all the necessary materials. He had approached a professional fly dresser some years earlier to ask about the best way to learn the art and had been told that 'it was impossible for an Amateur to acquire the art otherwise than by taking a series of lessons at a considerable cost'. Refusing to accept this, he had decided to teach himself and must have had some success with this as his first attempt, a Red Spinner, was good enough to fool an innocent grayling.

Now that he had met Marryat, his fly tying reached another level altogether and he 'soon found that [he] had acquired a means of giving [himself] a most pleasurable occupation during the long winter months'. Halford and a friend took rooms at Houghton Mill in 1880 'and there the work of learning and improving the method of fly dressing was initiated'.

But there was to be very much more to the collaboration between Halford and Marryat than learning how to tie flies, as Halford admitted. Serious collaboration between the two did not start until the autumn of 1881 when Halford started to seek Marryat's companionship as a fishing partner.

* * *

Dr Tom Sanctuary described Marryat, in 1879, as 'tall, spare, clean shaven, and bronzed, with a striking physiognomy'. Sanctuary had met Marryat on 15th March, 1879, for the first time for thirteen years as their paths had not crossed while Marryat was serving in the cavalry in India and then working in Australia. The day they met again, by the Old Barge in Winchester, was miserably cold, there was hardly any fly hatching and fishing was pretty hard going for little or no reward. Sanctuary 'noticed two fishermen having an animated discussion by the river side' and thought he recognised the taller of the two but struggled to put a name to the face. He felt certain that it was George Selwyn Marryat (whom he had always known as Selwyn) and to confirm this he went over and joined them. He commented to the one he thought to be Selwyn Marryat: "They take a bit more killing here than at Maiden Newton, don't they?"

"What do *you* know about the Frome at M. Newton?" was Selwyn's immediate reply.

"More than anyone who has fished it for several years," Sanctuary replied.

"Who the deuce *are* you then?" he queried. When Sanctuary revealed his identity, his old friend was equally delighted and immediately introduced him to his friend and fishing companion, Francis Francis.

Marryat and Francis had been arguing about how far it was possible to cast with an 11-foot single-handed rod. The two started casting with the same rod and both cast twenty-six yards. When Sanctuary took his turn, he managed a yard less. Sanctuary noted that there was no wind and that they were standing in the water meadow between Old Barge and Millpond, just above Waterman's Hut. This was the casting demonstration mentioned in a footnote in Francis' *A Book on Angling*.

Over the following years Sanctuary and Marryat spent a great deal of time in each other's company and between 1879 and 1887 Sanctuary maintained that Marryat's life was better known to him than any other friend or acquaintance who mourned his death. Many years after Marryat's death, Sanctuary wrote that he had 'stayed in years gone by' with him and Halford at Kimbridge when they fished the Test.

Sanctuary lived a long life, dying on 4th April, 1931, in Kirby Misperton on the river Costa, in Yorkshire, which he had fished since 1893. He started fishing the river not long after his arrival in the county having left Salisbury (where he lived in Crane Street) after he abandoned his wife and children in 1891. It seems likely that his arrival in Yorkshire was not an unmitigated blessing to the locals as he advised on the introduction of ranunculus to the Costa which then grew so extensively that it caused severe flooding and in the 1960s the river was described 'as a monument to the spoliation that can be done in the interests of drainage'.

Sanctuary was born in 1852, the son of Archdeacon Sanctuary who was the vicar of Powerstock in Dorset for many years. He had two younger brothers, Charles L. who went into the Church, and Campbell F. S. He started to learn to fish when he was about eight years old and some of his early fishing expeditions were with Selwyn Marryat's father Col. George Marryat and his family who lived close by at Mapperton House. Sanctuary was introduced to the dry fly when he was a pupil, aged fifteen, at Winchester, in April 1867, by John Hammond. In a letter to the *Fishing Gazette*, published in 1924, he wrote: 'John Hammond, the well-known Winchester fisherman, had initiated me into the art and mystery of making my fly float on the crystal waters of the Itchen, after I had completely failed to entice those wary trout by the usual two or three wet-fly means.' This was in the opening weeks of the season, before an Easter holiday spent fishing the Frome.

After Winchester, Sanctuary studied medicine at Edinburgh and following his qualification as a doctor, in 1878, he took a post as an Admiralty surgeon in Cornwall. Selwyn Marryat would stay with Sanctuary 'in Cornwall, for weeks at a time for the snipe and woodcock shooting'. Sanctuary married the next year and in 1883 he was living in Church House, Crane Street in Salisbury. He thoroughly enjoyed his invitations from Marryat and Halford to fish the Houghton Club's waters. On the river Test one August day he caught two big trout and two quality grayling when his hosts caught nothing. One can imagine that Marryat and Halford were probably too busy observing and collecting specimens of flies and yarning to worry too much about the fishing.

J. Bernard and Son, Jermyn Street, London, sold the Sanctuary Fly Rod, named after the doctor. The company's 1914 catalogue carried the rod which was described modestly as 'the finest dry-fly rod made, beautifully balanced, and very powerful in action'. The rod was available with two or three joints in lengths from 9-foot to 10-foot 6-inches and weights from 7oz to 9oz. The company's Test reels, either $3^1/_4$ inches or $3^1/_2$ inches were recommended to accompany the rods. Sanctuary also developed a fly pattern, known as the Sanctuary. When discussing smutting fish, Halford wrote: 'The Sanctuary on a large hook, a No. 1 or even No. 2, is more often taken by smutting grayling than trout.' The Sanctuary fly was number 54 in Halford's *Floating Flies and How to Dress Them* and the dressing was a body of dark hare's ear.

Many years later, particularly in about 1924 in correspondence to the *Fishing Gazette*, Sanctuary claimed he had been experimenting with oiling his flies to help them to float since 1867, the year he learnt to fish the dry fly. It must have been evident very quickly to the youthful Sanctuary that the flies he was trying to fish and keep dry needed some outside help. In 1924 he wrote: 'The Pope's nose, which I first used, was, as far as I can remember, from a fine fat bird and fit for the table, or he would not have been killed, so he was not deficient in oil.' He went on to describe how he re-greased his fly using 'whatever "greaser" I happen to be using', kept in a sovereign case 'with a piece of felt in each wing'. First he dried his fly, using a piece of amadou, and then pressed his fly into the felt, using 'a pencil end or something dry', and finally pinched the fly 'between the folds of my coat' to remove the surplus grease. But he was, he said, not particularly concerned about removing surplus grease. In another letter to the *Fishing Gazette* he described how to prepare lanolin, which was his favourite floatant, or if unavailable, neatsfoot oil. He had also used cod-liver oil, De Jong oil and other preparations.

Sanctuary moved to London in 1891 but it seems that although Marryat visited him there once in that year they saw each other rarely. Marryat did take his wife to London to visit the Fisheries Exhibition in May, 1883, but Sanctuary wrote that Marryat could tolerate the capital only for a day or two. His dislike of London may well have been an important consideration in his decision to refuse membership of the Fly-fishers' Club, a purely social and London-based club. Marryat wrote briefly of his visit to the 1883 exhibition in a letter to Henry Sinclair Hall (with whom he was to work on the development of eyed hooks suitable for fly fishing) on 11th July of that year: 'I went to the Exhib. with my Wife, but she liked the band, so I didn't see as much as if I had been alone, and it was nearly all in boxes when I was there. It is better now. I may run up and have a look at it later.' One of the official publications produced for the exhibition was a *Programme of Music, &c.* available at a cost of 2d or post-free 3d. Skues was also a visitor to the same exhibition and he noted that he saw 'specimens of floating flies [so] dressed by Mrs Cox [then of Winchester] and Mrs Brocas'. These 'beautifully tied split-winged floaters' which were 'so much better than the flies I had hitherto used' made quite an impression on him at what was the start of a long fishing career that was to blossom in the years following the exhibition. Incidentally, at the Fisheries Exhibition of 1896, held at the Royal Aquarium, on display on

George E. Holland's stand were examples of 'the late George Selwyn Marryat's last novelty in way of a design for Mayflies'.

The Great International Fishery Exhibition was held at South Kensington and was opened on 12th May by Queen Victoria. It ran for six months. Henry Wood gave organ recitals during the course of the exhibition.

Marryat's contemporaries described him as having a tall frame, long muscular arms and strong lissome fingers. He was known to be a strong, fit man who enjoyed excellent health, despite being a great pipe smoker - as depicted in a caricature drawn in 1893 by Basil Field. Pipes and cigars were smoked long into the night, accompanied by glasses of whisky and brandy, when Marryat and his chums were discussing and debating the angling pleasures and concerns of the day, particularly while staying at Houghton Mill. As well as his 'dry humour and reserves of knowledge', Major William Greer Turle wrote that 'he had a wonderful power of attraction to all who come under the sway of his genial manner and strong individuality'. Major Turle invented the eponymous knot that was one of the first - if not the first - for tying flies tied on eyed hooks to the gut cast, and was also one of 'her Majesty's servants' (a former soldier who had been badly wounded in Delhi during the Indian Mutiny) and a great fishing companion and host. R. B. Marston, then editor of the *Fishing Gazette*, was to write: 'I cannot imagine anyone preferring any knot to Major Turle's for eyed hooks for trout fishing'.

Marryat was said to be completely free of any personal deceit, arrogance or vanity, although his tam o'shanter was a significant gesture to unconventionality at a time when most fly fishermen still wore three-piece tweed suits, stiff collar and tie and much more formal headgear (interestingly, though, most photographs of Marryat do show him in a suit and collar and tie). To everyone who knew him, he was a genial, true-hearted friend and an unselfish fly fisherman. He was never a greedy fisherman and was often satisfied with two brace of fish a day and afterwards would return fish he caught to the river. This must have been one of the first examples of the practice, known today as catch and release, at a time when big bags were very much the order of the day and large catches were displayed on the bank and photographed for posterity. (There was at least one day when Marryat forgot himself and killed fourteen fish on the Test at Wherwell Priory.) One year when Halford was fishing for the first time that season at Kimbridge, on 3rd June, he had a 'hot and weary morning trying to get a fish wither with May-fly or Button' when he saw Marryat on the opposite bank. Marryat told Halford that he had killed his two brace of fish which weighed exactly 10lb and did not intend to fish any more that day. Marryat then joined Halford for a hurried lunch and afterwards the two set off together as Marryat 'had volunteered to yarn with me [Halford] until I had killed my two brace, when, as usual, we would both knock off'.

Marryat soon used his forcible character to impress upon Halford the necessity to acquire 'all available information in reference to the theory and practice of the dry fly'. Although Marryat was a far more knowledgeable and a more skilled fly fisherman than his peers, he knew that there was still a great deal to be learnt and it was not long before he and Halford began working together, writing down all the aspects that needed covering. These included: the selection of and handling of fly-tying materials; the practical aspects of fly casting; the nature and life cycle of the flies on the water; the correct choice of artificial fly according to the prevailing conditions and the time of the season; and even the improvement of rods, reels, fly lines and all the rest of the trout angler's tackle. 'Red Spinner' (William Senior) attributed 'the best improvements in rods, lines, winches [an old term for a fly reel], and flies' to Marryat.

Marryat and Halford worked together, and alone, on the Test and other rivers. They did much of their fieldwork on the life history of insects eaten by trout at Headbourne Worthy where they stayed in the cottage that Halford rented there until the end of 1890. They were, in particular, studying the life of the alder and they 'took many patches of eggs on the sedges, hatched them out, and after preserving a few specimens for future mounting, Marryat took a number back to Salisbury to try and rear them in his greenhouse'. Early on in their collaboration the two 'were most anxious that the scientific naming of them [the insects on which chalkstream trout fed] should be beyond question'. And to this end they consulted the leading authorities of the day including the Rev. A. E. Eaton 'one of the most eminent living entomologists'.

At this time Marryat was living in The Close, Salisbury, and he built himself a small aquarium and took soil and weed from the river Itchen in an endeavour to replicate as closely as possible the natural surroundings for his captive Alders. He kept the larvae until they were fully grown and managed to get two or three to pupate on a small piece of turf and then bred the imago. This work enabled Marryat and Halford to determine the life cycle of the species from egg to perfect insect at one year. Halford was to write that: 'As long as he [Marryat] lived we never relaxed our efforts to collect, examine, and check the classification from published works of all the specimens we could find.' Marryat impressed upon Halford that 'the only admissible proof of a particular insect serving as an article of food for the Salmonidae was finding them in the autopsy'. William Senior described the work involved and a typical autopsy in the chapter on 'Halford and His Contemporaries' in his book *Lines in Pleasant Places*: 'It meant the endless autopsy of fish and the patient searching of their entrails. To stand by while Halford and Marryat with their scissors, forceps, and whatnot laid out the contents of a trout's stomach, and bent low in separating and identifying the items, putting what were worthy of it under a microscope, and proceeding all the while as if the round world offered no other pursuit half so worthy of concentrated attention, was most fascinating. Many a time I was a spectator - I fear sometimes an irreverent one - of this ritual, but always privileged and welcome; always, of course, sympathetic, and always in a way envious of the qualities of mind and extraordinary knowledge which made the whole work a labour of love to them.' Of course, the two had the time to spend on their studies.

In contrast to what was to happen later, Marryat and Halford never departed from the understanding that they had arrived at together - that they would commit to paper the results of all their experiments, consider carefully their results and then verify them by further experiment. From the start of his collaboration with Marryat, Halford had 'decided to publish in some form, later on, for the benefit of the angling fraternity, all details we had worked out'. In 1899 when Halford reviewed his diary entries for an article in *Baily's Magazine*, December 1899, covering his first twenty-one years of fishing the chalkstreams, he wrote:

It had been my ambition for many years before to try to write a full handbook of the dry fly, and I was gratified to find that poor Marryat was quite in accord with me as to the need of such a work. He at once volunteered to render any assistance in his power, and this kindly offer was promptly and gratefully accepted. From that day to the end of his life we were continually in consultation either verbally or by correspondence.

After making notes and comparing our impressions for some years, he suggested that a full treatise on the subject would be a monumental work, and that it might be advisable to bring out as a ballot d'essai the fly-dressing portion in a separate volume. It was in furtherance of this idea that Floating Flies, and How to Dress Them, *was published in 1886, followed by* Dry-Fly Fishing in Theory and Practice, *in 1889. The publication of* Making a Fishery, *in 1895 and* Dry-Fly Entomology, *in 1897, completed the series of handbooks covering the ground of our original scheme.*

Unfortunately for Halford - and almost certainly for the development of fly fishing - Marryat would not countenance joint authorship which, in his opinion, would not be practicable. Halford, reluctantly and probably sadly, had to bow to his great friend's decision. H. S. Hall wrote that Marryat was free from 'anything like brag and ostentatious display' which may also have played a part in his refusal to be - and to be acknowledged publicly - the co-author of Halford's first book. When the original manuscript of *Floating Flies and How to Dress Them* was sold at auction in 2004, as well as notes in the margins from Halford, there were pencilled comments in Marryat's hand.

In the same article Halford wrote:

Some apology is due for devoting so much space to matters of a somewhat personal nature . . . Of the value of the co-operation of Mr Marryat it is needless to say anything - his knowledge, his experience, and his unselfish endeavour to assist are thoroughly appreciated by all of us. If these extenuating circumstances do not, in the reader's opinion, constitute a good and sufficient plea for leniency, perhaps a solemn pledge not to offend again - at least, not for the next twenty-one years - may serve to ward off the consequences of his wrath.

Marryat was consistent in committing almost nothing to print. R. B. Marston, editor of the *Fishing Gazette*, tried to get Marryat to write some articles on net making, a subject that

Marryat himself had suggested to Marston would make a good subject for publication. Marston wrote: 'I jumped at the suggestion, and by return of post asked him to do them. But he was not to be caught. No offer would tempt him to write.'

Although Marryat was an enthusiastic social letter writer (there was no other means of communication at this time), he appears to have written only two letters for publication, one published in *The Field,* 8th January, 1881, on quill bodies for dry flies and the second in the *Fishing Gazette*, 28th June, 1884, on the subject of who invented dry-fly fishing. And nothing else. No articles for *The Field* or the *Fishing Gazette* and no other letters. H. S. Hall wrote that he and Marryat 'kept up correspondence and interchange of ideas on all the *minutiae* of the fly fisher's craft', and 'what a fund of genial whit and humour was contained in his letters!' Hall was to write later of his regret that he never kept any of Marryat's letters. But according to Skues, writing many years later on the place of 'George Selwyn Marryat in the Evolution of the Modern Dry Fly' and published in the *Fly-Fishers' Club Journal* of 1923, 'Mr H. S. Hall gave me the most ungrudging aid from his records and correspondence, and among the letters which he lent me were several from G. S. Marryat'. Skues noted that Marryat was not very bothered about dating his letters but fortunately Hall had kept them all in their envelopes so he knew when they had been posted and used that information to date them.

2

Early Years

George Selwyn Marryat was the older son of a serving army officer, Lieut-Col. George Marryat (1806-1871), of the 23rd Regiment, and Georgiana Charlotte Marryat, née Selwyn (1816-1860). He was born on 20th June, 1840, at Chewton Glen ('Chuten' in some original documents), New Milton, in Hampshire, the third of ten siblings. He had six sisters: Agnes Charlotte, born in Kilmington in Somerset on 28th April 1837; Edith Mary Josephine, born in September 1838; Isabella L. in 1843; Amy Susan in September 1847; Rosalind Amelia in September 1850; and Eva Caroline in June 1853. He had three younger brothers: Herbert Charles, born on 6th May 1844; Alfred Henry, born on 26th February 1846; and Frederick Townsend, born on 4th August, 1855 at Mapperton House. Apart from Agnes Charlotte and Frederick Townsend, they were all born at Chewton Glen. Herbert Charles was educated in Jersey and followed his brother into the army. In April 1871 Lieut. Herbert Charles Marryat was an adjutant in the 96th Foot Regiment and eleven years later, in 1881, he was an unmarried captain in the Regiment (Active List Commanding

Officers' Militia) at the infantry barracks in Ashton Under Lyne. By 1901 he had retired from the army and was married to Emma Grace (née Caird) of Finnart, and they were living in Finnart House, Garelochhead in Dunbartonshire. All we know of Frederick Townsend is that he was married in Cambridge in the summer of 1878 and died on 17th March 1927. His wife had a volume of *Mummer Mystic Plays* published in 1900 by the New Century Press, London. Alfred Henry died in March 1863, not long after his seventeenth birthday, and was buried at St George's, Hanover Square, London.

When the Chewton Glen estate was sold in the early part of the twentieth century, the estate agents' particulars described it as follows: 'An exceptionally nicely situated and compact residential estate . . . The house, built in a delightful Georgian style, is of mellowed brick with tiled roof.' There was an entrance hall and reception hall, four reception rooms, servants' hall, kitchens, dairy and other domestic offices on the ground floor; eight principal bedrooms and three bathrooms on the first floor and three more bedrooms and five staff rooms on the second floor. Outside was a range of stabling, a walled kitchen garden and 'pleasure grounds' with four acres of woodland. The particulars also advised potential purchasers of 'the noted Chewton Glen stream which provides some small trout fishing'. Today Chewton Glen is a five-star country house hotel, spa and country club. Recent guests are said to have included the Rolling Stones. The house dates from the early 1700s but was remodelled in the Palladian style in the early 1890s. Colonel Marryat owned the house between 1837 and 1855 when it was bought by the Elphinstone family. The year after George's birth, 1841, his family was recorded staying in Richmond Terrace, off Whitehall, in Westminster. Ten years later the census for the night of 30th-31st March 1851, showed that George Selwyn was resident as a pupil at a school at Dacre Terrace, Lee in Kent,

Chewton Glen, New Milton, Hampshire. Birthplace of George Selwyn Marryat on 20th June, 1840. Marryat's family lived here before moving to Mapperton House.

Mapperton House in Dorset, once the home of Colonel George Marryat, Selwyn's father from 1854. The young Selwyn stared to fish the Frome at Maiden Newton when living here.

Shedfield Grange at the end of the nineteenth or early in the twentieth century. Marryat and his family lived there for ten years from 1874.

21 The Square, Winchester, (probably where John Hammond had his fishing tackle shop), where George Selwyn Marryat met F. M. Halford on 28th April, 1879.

Marryat and Sanctuary set up George Holland as a professional fly tyer at 96 Crane Street, Salisbury.

The river Avon in high summer, a few yards from George Holland's shop.

Above: Marryat may have travelled to Australia aboard the famous SS Great Britain.

Below: The river Darling and Bamamaroo lake (now Pamamaroo), part of the Menindee lakes system. Maryatt was appointed a magistrate of Menindee in April 1867. Painting by Ludwig Becker, 1860, copyright State Library of Victoria.

Opposite: Under the big poplars on the Houghton water. Photograph from Barton's An Album of the Chalkstreams.

Top: *The Abbots Barton Stretch of the Itchen.*
Above: *Boot Island, below Stockbridge on the Test*
Opposite: *May fly time on the Test.*

Photographs from Barton's An Album of the Chalkstreams.

tie down the old way —
half ... helled. now draw
the refuse fibre, down & back, half
on each side of the hook
and tie down behind
the wings along the hook
snip ... the balance to
the required taper — part
the hackle on hand up
to wings tie down & ... the
tail tie in whisks and

Part of a letter from Marryat describing his new method of tying up-wing dry flies.
From Side-Lines, Side-Lights & Reflections.

where the headmaster was a twenty-nine year old Maltese man with an English wife.

Marryat's sister Amy Susan married the Reverend Sir Hastings Bendall Baker, 3rd Baronet and son of Lieut-Col. Sir Edward Bendall Baker, the first Baronet, on 30th December 1875. She was his second wife and they had three daughters, Florence Laetitia, Olive Elizabeth and Eunice Evelyn and a son, Randolph Littlehales who died in 1959 aged eighty. She died on 26th January, 1940. Marryat's younger sister Eva Caroline died on 28th April 1943, was cremated and her ashes interred in Salisbury Cathedral Close where there is a small commemorative plaque in the ground. She appears not to have married as in 1901 she was single, living on her own means, with a woman servant, in London.

Edith Mary Josephine married Captain Charles Hamilton Malan on 21st August 1861 and they had one daughter, Evelyn Georgina. Edith died in 1866. Agnes Charlotte (a 'spinster and a gentlewoman') married George Edward Eliot ('gentleman') of Weymouth on 1st July, 1868, in the parish church at Mapperton. They had two children: Marion Edith, born 10th November, 1871, and Harold Selwyn, born nearly ten years later, on 20th April, 1881. The census of 1891 had the Eliots staying in Iwerne Courtney, Dorset, together with Agnes's sister Amy Susan and her husband Hastings Bendall Baker. In 1901 Agnes was a patient in St Thomas' Hospital in London. She died in Bicester in 1919. Isabella is recorded at the age of thirty-eight, in 1881, as a Sister of Mercy at the Convent of Holy Trinity, Woodstock, in Oxfordshire.

Selwyn's father was a younger brother of Captain Frederick Marryat (1792-1848) - the second son of Joseph and Charlotte Marryat who produced the astonishing number of fifteen children, ten of whom survived. Joseph's sons were described as being 'full of wildness, waggishness and worth'. Frederick

Marryat had a miserable time at school and ran away time after time. After one escapade, his father gave him some money and sent him back to school in a hackney cab. The cab arrived at the school, but it was empty. Frederick had escaped from the cab into the street and was found later that evening 'enjoying himself hugely in the company of numerous brothers and sisters at a pantomime'.

Marryat's fishing career started to blossom following his family's move to Mapperton House, Dorset (mid-way between Bridport and Crewkerne) in 1854. The move may have had something to do with the West Country branch of the Marryat family who claimed to be descended from a Norman family that had arrived in England with William the Conqueror and acquired land in Somerset. Pevsner's *The Building of England, Dorset,* starts its description of Mapperton with the words 'There can hardly be anywhere a more charming manorial group than Mapperton. Part of the charm lies in the vagueness about what is public and what private'. The manor of Mapperton is said to be one of Dorset's oldest and at the time of the Domesday Book it was owned by the sheriff of Somerset, William de Moion. The current house was built in Ham stone by Robert Morgan in the 1540s taking in an existing house and like many historic buildings has been extended over the years, with new wings and many other features, both internal and external, particularly in the 1670s when it was enlarged. It was in the ownership of just four families, inherited through the female line, until 1919. When the Marryats lived there it was owned by the Compton family of Minstead. Henry Combe Compton MP was Tory Member of Parliament for South Hants for twenty-two years. Mapperton House is now the home of the Earl and Countess of Sandwich whose family has owned the house since 1955.

Selwyn Marryat's parents and four sisters, a governess and a number of servants were still living at Mapperton House at the time of the 1861 census, held on 7th and 8th April. His mother was not included in the census return as she had died the previous year. George Selwyn did not appear either as he was in India in the army.

It was while living at Mapperton House that Selwyn started to fish the Frome at Maiden Newton, to the north-west of Dorchester. He, together with his father and brother (whom Sanctuary described as 'the present Major Marryat'), were three noted wet-fly fishermen and Selwyn 'was named "the Otter" by the local rustics, and no bad name either'. This was in the days before the dry fly had arrived in Dorset. Sanctuary and the Marryats had leave to fish the best parts of the Frome and Marryat's father taught Sanctuary to spin for trout with a minnow, casting up and across.

After leaving the army and following his return from Australia in 1869, George Selwyn went to live with his parents. By now he was thirty years old, his father was sixty-four. He was listed as a lieutenant in the cavalry. At this time the family were living on Pulteney Road in the parish of Bathwick in Bath. On 9th July, 1872 George Selwyn married Lucy Dorothea Clinton, daughter of Col. Frederick Clinton (Grenadier Guards) of Ashley Clinton, Hampshire (which was very near to where he had been born), and the Hon. Margaret Clinton (*née* Scott-Montagu). The wedding took place at the church of St George, Hanover Square, London. His new wife, Lucy Clinton, had been born in Eaton Place, London, in 1843, but had been living in Hampshire, at Shedfield Cottage, since at least 1851. At some point before or just after their marriage, the Marryats moved to Edinburgh, to 19 Hope Terrace, and later that year, on 26th November 1872, George Selwyn wrote a new will from that address leaving everything to his new wife. They did not spend very long in Scotland as, at the end of 1874, they moved to Hampshire where they lived at Shedfield Grange, Sandy Lane, Shedfield, to the east of Southampton on the edge of the Meon valley. They remained here for about ten years. Shedfield was a village built on the last surviving fragment of open heath-land that had stretched between the Itchen and the Sussex border. It was then a very rural part of Hampshire where the soils were not very good for farming.

Selwyn's sisters Rosalind Amelia and Eva Caroline also lived in Shedfield in the early 1880s, at Shedfield Cottage. Rosalind was head of the household and when the census of 1881 was held, the two sisters' four-year old niece Alice Baker and her one-year old brother, Randolph, were in residence. They were the children of their sister Amy Susan.

Marryat rented Shedfield Grange, which has five bedrooms, from Admiral Augustus Phillimore who lived at Shedfield House. A memo of agreement to let Shedfield Grange 'with the orchard gardens, small coachhouse and stable for a horse attached to it', drawn up by Marryat and signed, sealed and dated 9th December, 1875, noted that the house had previ-ously been occupied by a shepherd. The rental agreement for 3rd October, 1881, detailed that the annual rental of £65 was payable at Lady Day and Michaelmass. The adjoining farmyard was not included in the agreement. Marryat agreed to rent the house from 1st January 1876 until 1884 when, on 5th Novem-ber, he wrote to Admiral Phillimore to confirm that he had found a house in The Close, Salisbury and that he understood that 'Mrs Marryat' had given the required six months' notice to Mrs Phillimore. He told the Admiral that he was prepared to leave the house 'short after Christmas' should any friend of the Admiral wish to take it after him. Marryat also advised his land-lord that he was waiting to hear from a friend, Capt. Travis, who had 'expressed a wish to know if we are leaving'. He expected to hear from him in the course of a day or two. Before he left for Salisbury, Marryat had some items in the kitchen valued officially, by a local auctioneer, comprising a painted dresser near the window, with sliding doors under and open shelves over, another dresser with two drawers and under cupboards and open shelves over, a cupboard nearest the door, the kitchen range and a cupboard with folding doors in the pantry. The valuation of £17/7/6 was dated 19th January, 1885.

The Marryat's first daughter, Mary Margaret, was born in Shedfield in 1876, on 3rd August, followed by Dorothea Charlotte Edith on 16th December, 1881, also at Shedfield Grange, and, in 1883, their last, Joan O. Gladstone who was born in London. There was another daughter, Alice Lucy, who was born on 12th May, 1877, but she did not live for very long and died the following year on 4th April, having suffered from nephritis (inflammation of the kidneys) for four days. While living at Shedfield Grange, Marryat and his wife employed four servants. About two years after the birth of their last daughter Joan, they moved to The Close, Salisbury where they employed five servants including a cook, parlourmaid, housemaid, a governess for the children and a gardener.

Shedfield was quite handy for getting to the Itchen, which he fished with Francis Francis between 1879 and 1882, but a little less handy for the Test. While he was living at Shedfield Grange, Marryat was a member, number thirty-two, of the Dorchester Fishing Club which was founded in 1877 when water was leased from the Duchy of Cornwall. Marryat was a member for only one season, that of 1879. The Dorchester Fishing Club fished the same waters as the earlier Dorchester Angling Club which was formed in 1845. Today the club has about seven miles of wild brown trout and grayling fishing, extending below and above Dorchester, on the Frome and the Cerne, together with various carriers and side streams.

In a letter written from Shedfield Grange, postmarked 11th

July, 1883, Marryat wrote to H. S. Hall: 'Categorically to you I fared middling on the Mayfly but it didn't come up till the 1st June and then I had to take my Mrs to "her Ma's".' This was on the 2nd when he 'Took Mrs M to Ashley and 2 kids'. As he did not record having fished on the 3rd, one can assume that his visit involved two days. In spite of this distraction, he still managed to fish on thirteen of the first eighteen days of the month. There was no mention of the 10th, he did not fish on the 14th as it was too hot and he went home to 'Shedfield' on the 15th.

As already mentioned, Marryat's great friend and fishing companion was Francis Francis. Born Francis Morgan at Seton, Devon, Francis was the son of Capt. Morgan, RN. His mother was the only daughter of Henry Robinson Hartley who founded the Hartley Institution in Southampton. During his childhood his father was away at sea and his mother was 'too great an invalid to have a boy much with her'. He had only a sister who died young. As one of the terms of the will of his step-grandfather, Mr Francis who had left him some property, Francis Morgan adopted the surname of his step-grandfather on coming of age. Although he was described as coming from 'genuine sailor stock' and 'a typical sailor in manner and appearance', Francis had no great love of the sea. The memoir of Francis Francis in the sixth edition of *A Book on Angling* (published in 1885) described his appearance as 'Five feet eight inches in height, with perfect limbs, broad shoulders, and a chest measurement of forty-six inches, the bronze visaged old sportsman was a model of strength, and possessed an iron constitution. His hair was jet black, his eyes true blue; but both eyes and hair lost much of their colour before he died'.

Having been educated at various private schools and by private tutor, Francis refused to go to college, deciding instead to become a civil engineer. Although he finished his articles he never practised and 'thenceforward devoted himself to sport and sporting literature'. He was married in 1851 and had three sons and three daughters. He was described as 'A fair classical scholar, and thoroughly intimate with English standard literature, he painted and sang well, was at one time a creditable musician, a good whip and cricketer, a fine shot, good at billiards and smart with the "gloves", a whist-player of force, and learned in horticulture. His taste for whist and gardening he preserved to the end. Shrewd businessmen who knew him well have often said that, had he been forced to depend upon his own exertions for a living, his extraordinary energy, inventive faculties, fertility of resource, and decision would assuredly have won him a large fortune. Be this as it may, with a concentration that steadily increased as he grew older, angling and matters relating to that craft drew him more and more absorbingly from other pursuits.' An impatient man in everything but angling, Francis described himself as having the untiring patience of a Red Indian in all matters piscatorial.

The only acknowledgement Francis Francis received for a lifetime spent managing and promoting the interests of angling, was an opossum rug sent to him by some Australian anglers in appreciation of his work in establishing the brown trout in that country. His work as angling editor of *The Field*, from 1856 to 1883, was not well remunerated either, but for all the years that Irwin Cox, one of the proprietors of *The Field*, rented a stretch of the Itchen, the angling editor of the publication had standing leave to fish there. Francis was initially paid £2 a column but that was changed to an annual salary of £200. No doubt his inheritance and investments meant that such a small salary was not an impediment to his retaining the post for as long as he was physically able. The memoir made the point that he worked for the love of it and would, in all probability, have done it for nothing. For a passionate and committed all-round angler, he seems to have led a wonderful life. As well as the many fishing books, articles and novels he wrote, he left a large amount of unpublished matter consisting of 'plays, burlesques, poetry, and stories'. He wrote quickly and easily and was never unemployed.

Francis was also, for some years, naturalist director of the Brighton Aquarium, a position that 'afforded [him] special opportunities of observing the habits of the salmon (British)'. He included in the sixth edition of his famous work *A Book on Angling* much of what he had learnt from his observations at the aquarium and maintained that it formed 'the most complete history of the subject at present existing'. Although Francis and Marryat helped develop an oil dressing for silk fly lines and other innovations in fishing tackle, he could not be persuaded to move away from his favourite long, heavy double-handed trout rods at a time when trout anglers were starting to use shorter and slightly lighter single-hand rods.

Francis's career and life came to a sad end when he had a severe stroke in 1883 which finished his work as an editor and an author. In fact his last contribution to *The Field* was published on 13th July, 1883. In 1885 he managed to leave his home in Twickenham and fish the Itchen at Winchester in May and he had a week of grayling fishing at Houghton in August. His last outing with a fly rod was in October the next year, barely two months before his death on 24th December, 1886, from a recurrence of cancer of the tongue for which he had been operated on twice. The paralysis from his stroke, illness and wasting caused by the cancer 'had reduced him to but the saddest shadow of his former self'. His work for *The Field* gave him 'peculiar facilities for obtaining permission to fish very many waters which are closely locked against the general public'. He roamed far and wide over England, Scotland and Wales gleaning fresh knowledge wherever he went. Much of this knowledge formed the basis of his best-known work, *A Book on Angling*.

A footnote on the first page of the chapter on 'Artificial Fly-Fishing', notes his involvement with the first successful shipment of trout ova to Australia (see Chapter 4, Adventures in Australia). Another footnote in the same chapter records his 'friend Mr Marryat' casting a single-hand rod twenty-six yards on the Old Barge river. Although the names of a number of contemporary angling writers and owners of fishings are included by Francis, the footnote seems to be the only mention of Marryat in his book of over five hundred pages.

One of his last articles, published in the book *Angling Reminiscences* and previously in *The Field* of 16th June, 1883, was 'The Mayfly Mess' which he wrote in 1883. In the article he wrote about fishing the Mayfly, with Marryat, on their own waters of the Itchen in a constant north-east gale which was to ruin the whole Mayfly season. Readers who are not fully aware of the delights and challenges of fly fishing for trout, may not appreciate the difficulties that can be caused by fishing when a strong downstream wind is blowing. These difficulties are still the same today but were amplified in Victorian times by the relative inefficiencies of the tackle that even the best anglers of the day had at their disposal. The chalkstreams of Hampshire flow, essentially, from north to south and as dry-fly fishermen had now started to fish upstream, this meant that they had to cast into the wind. Casting into a wind, particularly a strong one, affects how far a fly can be cast and the accuracy of a cast. A gust of wind at the wrong time will catch your fly and blow it away from its intended target. As well as having to cope with casting into the wind, gusts of wind blowing over the surface of the water make it difficult to see the fish below the surface. Strong winds also affect flies on the surface of the river, more so the big ones such as Mayflies, which get blown about and are sometimes even capsized by a good blast. Some years later Sanctuary complained of the Mayfly season on the Nidd, in

Yorkshire, being ruined by strong and cold east winds.

On one day Marryat fished the main river and caught two and a half brace of trout, including one fish which went to nearly three pounds and two of about two pounds, while Francis caught only one, of about two and a half pounds in a cross stream where the wind was not such a nuisance. One Tuesday Francis and Marryat fished their own waters of the Itchen, following a morning spent walking and yarning until about two o'clock. Towards the end of the same day Francis caught another fish on 'a very artistic spent gnat' he had that had been 'tied by friend M'. Later he was to write that M's spent gnats 'have done better by far than any other this season'. Francis also wrote that 'The Mayfly season at Winchester has been an utter failure. That N.E. gale broke the back of it and choked the fish off, and they never recovered . . . There was no heartiness in the rise, and they never took the natural fly at all freely; and as for the way they shammed at the artificial, it was awful.' Marryat was a great joker and enjoyed playing schoolboy pranks on his fishing companions. This day was no exception and when one of three more trout that he caught was 'a beast as long as an eel . . . he slyly dropped [it] into my [Francis's] basket'. It was, obviously, a fish that had still to recover fully from the rigours of spawning and put on weight and condition.

Like Marryat himself, Francis was great company and 'Witty, cheerful, bright full of anecdote and jest, with a laugh that did a man's heart good, as a young man he was the life and soul of any company that he entered, and despite the sobering influence of age was eminently good company to the last'.

* * *

Marryat won a scholarship to Winchester College in 1854 and College boys were able to fish the river Itchen when the school curriculum allowed the necessary free time (although, as we shall see, the school day was not organised to aid the tyro fly fisher). The College had owned (and still owns) parts of the Itchen since the fourteenth century and Winchester boys were able to fish about half a mile of it, known as Old Barge, in return for a small annual payment. One fellow Winchester pupil, Edward Grey (Viscount Grey of Fallodon), wrote at some length and with eloquence on the subject of fly fishing on the Itchen in his book *Fly Fishing* and from his accounts we can learn a great deal about school life for the ardent fly fisher there, and what it must have been like for Marryat. In the early 1950s some of the water meadows adjoining the Itchen were named the Fallodon Reserve in Grey's memory (he died in 1933).

Lord Grey started his first term at Winchester in September 1876, about a fortnight before the end of the trout season, but his first weeks were so strange as he settled in that he did not think about fishing. Although this was over twenty years after Marryat started his education there, he gives us a good account of what life was like then for a Winchester school boy determined to fish as much as possible. Skues, when in his last year at Winchester, remembered seeing 'Grey as a small boy in Eton jacket, grey trousers, and a straw hat with the distinguishing ribbon of Du Boulay's House'. As Skues did not fish in 1877 (his last season), due to time spent preparing for his exams, he did not meet Grey while he was still at school.

The name Skues has cropped up a number of times and although he is not a central character in this book, his name will re-appear on more than one occasion. This might suggest that a footnote would suffice to say who he was but George Edward Mackenzie Skues was far too important a character in the development of fly fishing, and particularly nymph fishing, to be consigned to a mere footnote. For those readers unfamiliar with his name, Skues was born in 1858 in Newfoundland where his father was surgeon of the Newfoundland Companies.

He arrived in England aged three. Although he fished during his time at Winchester College 'with an impossible rod and line and with flies supposed to be fished dry but in build best suited to be fished downstream wet', his fishing career did not really get started until after his visit to the Fisheries Exhibition of 1883. Skues trained and worked as a solicitor in London. During a very long life spent fishing the Itchen most of the time, he had difficulty accepting the strict code of the dry fly as laid down by Halford and is now known as the father of fishing the upstream nymph. His enthusiasm for fishing nymphs during the early decades of the twentieth century, particularly on rivers where the dry fly was considered the only acceptable way of catching trout, was highly controversial and he and Halford had many disagreements. It also led to his giving up his rod on the Itchen. Skues never received during his lifetime the adulation that Halford did. It must be said that he did not seek it nor did he hold court in hotels at the end of a day's fishing as did Halford. He was a fairly harsh reviewer of some of Halford's books although in his article on the life and fishing career of Halford, published in the *Salmon and Trout Magazine* in 1929, he did go some way towards retracting some of his harsher criticisms. Skues was a prolific author of both books and articles himself, the latter published under a range of pseudonyms in various magazines and journals. He eventually hung up his rod at the grand old age of eighty-seven when he was living in an hotel in Wiltshire.

Grey was to make plans during the winter for the opening of the trout season the following year. He soon discovered that the Itchen trout were to be seen feeding very easily in the clear waters of the river and were bigger in size than any that he had caught in the 'burns of my north country home' in Northumberland. He was told that these fish were very difficult to catch and 'that with few exceptions no one at school ever had caught any'.

The school day at Winchester was such that it placed a pre-
mium on time management for the young angler. Boys were
not set free from the classroom until midday and had to return
to their house 'for dinner' one hour later; attendance was com-
pulsory although it was possible to be a few minutes late
without attracting attention. Unfortunately for the young Grey,
his house - Du Boulay's in Edgar Street - was the furthest but
one from the river. (Marryat's house was College, in College
Street, which was that bit closer to the river.) Thus there was no
time for Grey to return from the main school buildings to his
house to collect his tackle. Doing so would have lost him at
least ten minutes on the riverbank. 'It was necessary to make
arrangements by which one could rush from school at twelve
o'clock without a moment's delay, with rod and tackle ready
for immediate use, and with things of some kind on one's feet
and legs, which, even when the water was "out", would with
ordinary care keep dry inside in the water meadows.' It was
important to try to keep one's feet dry as there was no time to
change footwear before dinner and the prospect of spending
the rest of the afternoon with wet feet did not appeal, even to
a fourteen-year old boy. If the 'dons' were punctual in bringing
work to an end, Grey could be fishing within about five minutes. It was his good fortune to be able to fish this hour which
he came to believe to be the most profitable hour of the fishing
day.

On 'whole school days' it was not possible to fish for the full
hour but there was more time on half-holidays although there
were rarely any fish rising at that time. In the summer, boys
were allowed to fish in the evenings but as they had to be
indoors by eight o'clock sharp, they often missed the best of
the evening rise. 'There was more discipline to be learnt in this
way than in any other at school. To have a passion for fishing,
to spend an hour by the river evening after evening watching

intently for a rising trout, and invariably to tear oneself away just as the rise began, was a curious experience.' As well as fishing Old Barge (which had been a canal in the previous century, used to move coal and corn to and from Southampton), boys were allowed to fish on New Barge along the old towpath above Shawford and 'from one side under the elm trees at St Cross'. As these stretches of water were further away from the college, Marryat and then later Grey and his chums fished them only on free afternoons, and then only if there were no trout to be seen rising on Old Barge. A photograph, possibly taken by Marryat, as some were, of Old Barge in Halford's *An Angler's Autobiography*, shows a solid line of trees on one bank, which look virtually unfishable, and a good path - at one time the towpath one presumes - and adjoining meadows on the other bank. Red Spinner (William Senior) wrote in his obituary of Marryat published in the *Fishing Gazette* that 'the camera proved a fascination to him, and he took many trout streams views that would be, to the frequenter of Itchen and Test, priceless. A mutual friend recently showed me some albums he has of such views, produced with a softness and beauty which are unsurpassed.'

As soon as Grey arrived at Old Barge he would choose an unoccupied spot where fish were rising and stay there for the duration. On the opening day of his first season, 1st March 1877, 'Surely no one ever fished the Itchen with greater anticipation and with less chance of success'. The water meadows were under water and he had only thin, un-greased boots. He fished with 'a whippy double-handed rod of some thirteen feet in length, and three flies, probably a March-brown, a Coch-y-bondu and a Greenwell's Glory, which I generally used in those days'. He did not think of casting to a rising fish but fished the water steadily. He left the water reluctantly, wet but still keen even though he had fished without a touch. 'The same thing happened day after day, nothing occurred to break the monotony of failure, and my friends ceased even to ask whether I had caught anything.' As we will see later on, it is very likely that Marryat fished only wet flies while he was a 'commoner', as Winchester College pupils are known, as he did not start fishing dry flies until some years later.

In his book *Chalkstream and Moorland, Thoughts on Trout-Fishing*, written 'with the avowed object of amusing rather than teaching', Harold Russell included the following on the early days of dry-fly fishing: 'Some little while since an article in *The Field* on the origin of the dry-fly evoked some interesting letters from old Wykehamists, who remembered the Itchen half a century ago. We have the evidence of one, whose memory went back to the years 1844 to 1848, that the systematic use of the dry fly, as we know it, was unknown at that time on the Winchester College water. The boys had only a short time for fishing, but they used to look for a rise and made a point of putting their fly, while it was still dry, over the trout. After a few casts it got soaked, and they went on fishing in the usual way. On changing flies they gave the new fly a similar chance by floating it over a rise. Occasionally a man would change flies merely to get a dry one. The extraordinary thing is that, having got so far, no one discovered that by whisking the fly briskly through the air it was possible to keep it dry and make it float.' But writing about the Itchen a few years later in the 1860s '. . . if we are to believe old Wykehamists, no one thought of employing any other method than dry-fly. Flies were got from Hammond in those days, and they were tied to float with upright wings.'

But success did come for Grey one day when he hooked a tiny trout at the very bottom of the water. However it was still early in the season when very few anglers were on the river. But when the local anglers who knew the river started to appear on the banks, Grey was able to watch how they fished and ask them questions. He bought himself some flies from John Hammond and it was with one of these flies that he caught his first takeable Itchen brown trout in June. It was the only fish of any size that he caught all season. But it was a rising fish and was caught on a Red Quill Gnat. He was now able to give a positive response to those who asked whether he had *ever* caught anything!

Grey wrote, as quoted above, of the water meadows being under water. Water meadows were a very important aspect of the management of rivers and the adjoining grass fields and meadows. In Grey's time they were worth 50/- (£2.50) an acre in rent. The famous chalkstreams of Hampshire, Wiltshire and Dorset had been modified and developed in the seventeenth and eighteenth centuries to provide water for flooding the riverside meadows to improve their productivity. This work was done by farm workers known as 'drowners'. Water was impounded and then when the river had reached a suitable level, the water would be released through a series of sluices into a network of carriers and ditches and allowed to be over-topped so that the surrounding grassland was flooded. The marshes would be flooded for between twenty-four and forty-eight hours, at the end of which, the various sluices would be opened so that the marshes could be drained and the floodwater returned to the main river. The first flooding of the year would be in February or March, as experienced by Grey at the start of the season, when the temperature of the river water was higher than that of the land and this would encourage the grass to grow quickly, ready to be grazed a few weeks later by sheep and cattle. Skues wrote that the whole of the valley of the Itchen, between the hills on either side, except for the river, side streams and its carriers and a few copses, was all farmed by irrigation. The grass was either grazed by fattening cattle or made into hay with two and sometimes even three crops being taken during the season. The meadows were drowned after each cut of hay to encourage the grass to grow.

After they were grazed by sheep in April and May, the meadows were flooded again to produce a crop of hay. Hay was cut in July after which the meadows were grazed by cattle until the end of November. During the winter the dykes were cleaned out, ready to flood the meadows again. The drowners' activities were not always popular with anglers due to the effect that the flooding and subsequent release of water had on water levels in the rivers and carriers.

Halford had one or two harsh things to say about drowners and their work in his first book *Dry-Fly Fishing, Theory and Practice* (dedicated originally to 'George Selwyn Marryat' by his 'grateful pupil'). He refers to them when writing about the management of a fishery and the problem of poachers and in his opinion drowners, 'the men regulating the water in the meadows, have exceptional opportunities of taking the large fish out of carriers or small drains at night or early morning. They run up these drains to feed on worms, and a small landing-net is all that is required to take them out.' Surely a competent river keeper would have been fully appraised of their habits and opportunities to poach large trout?

Day tickets were also issued for Old Barge and Grey recorded that he had seen as many as eleven rods fishing at the same time. The average number of rods during the best parts of the season was around four or five. In his tribute to Marryat, who he had met for the first time in 1868, in the *Fishing Gazette*, Major Turle remarked that Old Barge 'would have been a really good piece of water if old John Hammond, who rented it, had not crammed in so many rods, or the weeds had grown less luxuriantly, fed by the town sewage, which at that time was allowed to find its way into the river'. This level of fishing pressure had the inevitable results on the fish which became very difficult to catch. Grey maintained that they were not that shy - you could approach them relatively easily - and it 'was possible to go on casting for hours over rising trout without putting them down'.

Many well-known anglers of the day fished Old Barge, including Francis Francis whom Grey described as 'probably the best known of all authorities on angling' and also Marryat 'the greatest angler I have ever met'. Of the latter, Grey wrote, 'One could not say which was the more instructive, to watch his fishing or to listen to his talk; no one had more information to give, no one was more generous in giving it'. Grey felt that Marryat had a 'peculiar insight' into the ways of trout as well as being a keen observer. His recollections of Marryat included the way that he managed his rod and tackle which demonstrated not only his practical skill but his genius as well. Following Marryat's death and being aware of all the tributes that had been published, he wrote an article in the *Fishing Gazette* in which he acknowledged that Marryat's genius 'was widely recognised, most highly estimated, and most willingly deferred to by those who knew him best'.

In the same issue of the *Fishing Gazette*, H. S. Hall described an encounter between Marryat and a College boy fishing on the Old Barge stream. 'Marryat's extraordinary skill with the fly rod was well known all over the chalkstream country. One of the most remarkable things about him was the way in which he could pick up another man's rod and tackle and do better work with it than the owner himself was capable of. One morning in May, 1881, we were strolling together by the Old Barge stream at Winchester, and just below the bathing place we found one of the College boys fishing over a free-rising trout. We had watched in silence for some time, when suddenly Marryat walked up, and, in his characteristic way, accosted the angler with, "Here my son, give me that rod." In less than a minute the fish was hooked, and the rod handed back to the astonished owner.'

Grey, like Marryat and Skues, had a life-long affection for Winchester and had encouraged his old school to start a fishing club which leased some fishing on the Itchen. The club was formed in 1905 when the Warden and Fellows leased the rights to the School Fishing Association. Today the College owns about four and a half miles, both banks, of the Itchen. The fishing club is open to all boys - who can fish three days a week - during term time, and Old Wykehamists can fish during the holidays. (Well-known angler and author Sidney Vines claims that Lord Grey was approached and provided the necessary finance.)

Interestingly, that other great Winchester fly fisher, Skues, never met Marryat. As a pupil at Winchester, Skues (who was born in 1858) saw Marryat at the annual cricket match against Eton but was, by his own admission, too shy to go and speak to the great master. What a missed opportunity! Skues wrote in 1918 that at a time when 'tall hats and frock coats were de rigueur' Marryat would 'stalk into New Field in his pepper and salt knicker-bocker suit and woollen tam o'shanter', which he described many years later as 'festooned with Mayflies'. While one can understand Skues' reluctance as a schoolboy to approach Marryat, it does seem strange that they never met on the riverbank in later life as they shared mutual fishing friends and fished the same rivers, although Skues did spend more time fishing the Itchen than Marryat. If the two had met, who knows how the history of fly fishing for trout might have been affected. Would Marryat have vouchsafed to Skues that he and Halford had experimented with artificial nymphs? If he did not, would Skues' work on the development of nymph fishing have affected Marryat and encouraged him to spend more time fishing below the surface? One of the problems of understanding how

Marryat fished is that most of the information comes from Halford and his writing. Marryat's peers who fished at the same time, and with him, were much influenced by Halford who was also a friend and regular fishing companion to many of them. Once Halford and Marryat had eschewed the nymph in their own angling, Halford would not have mentioned again any further fishing with nymphs. At this time nymph fishing was not that well understood, although it was to be some time in the future before many of those who attempted to fish with them were likely to be ostracised as little better than poachers.

3

The Carabiniers

As Marryat was the son of an army officer and a nephew of Captain Frederick Marryat, the naval officer and well-known Victorian novelist, it is not surprising that he joined the army too. His uncle was a most interesting character and it is a shame that he died when George Selwyn was so young (in 1848); they shared a number of characteristics but Selwyn was never able to get to know him. Capt. Marryat has been described as 'England's most famous author in the years between Jane Austen and Charles Dickens' but that was only one aspect of the man. In his biography of him, Tom Pocock, writing about his suitability as a husband, noted that he was 'a well-to-do naval hero and son of a prominent financier and politician; strikingly handsome: square jawed and merry-eyed; broad shouldered and deep chested'. On his retirement from the navy he had shown a seeming ability to be able to adapt to a number of different roles including evolving from naval officer to a man-about-town, a good father, author and country gentleman. But if 'his practicality, charm and humour proved unable or inappropriate, he could, like "Gentleman Chucks", become harsh, even, violent and the fuse of his temper was short'. He was frightened of no one and once ended-up in court and fined for brawling in the streets.

Frederick Marryat was left two very substantial sums of money, one by his father and the other by his Uncle Samuel who had been a lawyer. His father (Selwyn's grandfather) has been described as a merchant prince who was head of the banking house of Marryat, Kaye, Price & Co.; member and later chairman of the committee of Lloyd's; colonial agent for the islands of Trinidad and Grenada; and an MP, first for Horsham and then for Sandwich. Frederick was a man of charm and wit, impetuous and extravagant, who made and then wasted large sums of money from his writing. As a man-about-town he lived in London and also had a house in Brighton where he attended soirées held by George IV at the Royal Pavilion. At these gatherings he regaled the assembled company with tales of his time in Burma and told many other stories and jokes. In contrast to his nephew, who was also a good storyteller, Frederick Marryat loved London and was quite happy to play the part of entertainer when required.

Frederick Marryat was appointed a gentleman-in-waiting to the Duke of Sussex who, in return, offered him the lease of Sussex House on Fulham Palace Road, London. Then in 1830 'In London one night, over a bottle of champagne and, perhaps, either in tipsy bravado, or in a gamble, with a rich builder and architect, Alexander Copland, he had exchanged the handsome Sussex House, for a farm of a thousand acres on the coast of Norfolk'. Although he lived there at times and ran the farm - losing money for many years - his literary and other friends were reluctant to visit him in rural Norfolk. His daughter Florence was to describe his attempts at being a farmer as: 'Captain Marryat tried very hard to be a regular farmer, but . . . he was a farmer in theory only and not in practice.' He then let the farm for a number of years before returning to Norfolk in 1843. Towards the end of his life he had a recurrent health problem. He was refused a pension by the Admiralty and promptly 'exploded with frustration and anger' and suffered internal haemorrhages 'necessitating a return to Norfolk for recuperation'. Subsequently he never recovered from the shock of hearing that his eldest son had died in a shipwreck. He died on his Norfolk farm on 9th August, 1848, at the age of fifty-six. He was buried in the churchyard of St Andrew in Langham. His will was proved on 25th October, 1848, and the value of his estate was £9,000. He entrusted the care of his daughters to his sister Ellen and brother George (Selwyn's father).

His novels for both adults and children were bestsellers in their day. Some such as *Children of the New Forest* are still popular and his famous sea stories, for example, *Frank Mildmay* and *Mr Midshipman Easy* were the founders of a fictional genre of which C. S. Forester and Patrick O'Brian are modern descendants. As a boy he went to sea with Lord Cochrane - the most dashing frigate captain of them all - and saw much action. He fought the Americans in 1812 and was then lionised by them as a celebrated author only to be reviled later for helping to suppress a French-Canadian rebellion. His books were based on his experiences and travels including an extended tour of America.

The Captain, who lived apart from his wife for much of his life, had eleven children. His son Samuel Francis, Frank, also became a published author. Frank was born in 1826 and died in 1855. The Captain's daughter Augusta, who was known as Gussy, wrote and illustrated children's stories as did her sisters Blanche and Emily. Florence was a prolific novelist, singer and comedy actress who also wrote about spiritualism and ghosts, including the ghost at Raynham in Norfolk. She was married twice (first to Major Gen. T. Ross Church in her late teens, and then to Colonel Francis Lean) and died on 27th October, 1899. In 1895 she made a successful lecture tour in the USA, and she opened a school of literary art in February 1897. Lieut. Frederick Marryat, George Selwyn's eldest cousin, at the age of twenty-eight was second lieutenant on *HM Avenger* (a first class steam frigate of 1441 tons) which was wrecked in a storm on the Sorelle Rocks, near Galatia, in the Mediterranean on 20th December, 1847. This event was indicative of the fact that sailing anywhere in the middle and later decades of the nineteenth century was still a hazardous undertaking and George Selwyn, who was to sail to India and later to Australia, was fortunate not to have shared the same fate as his cousin.

On completion of his education at Winchester, George Selwyn joined the Carabiniers (6th Dragoon Guards), a relatively senior regiment, as a cornet, on 16th March, 1858. At a time when it was still the accepted practice for those with the necessary funds to buy a commission he joined without purchase in succession to Lieut. Hudson who had been killed in action.

Cornet Marryat left Maidstone on completion of his initial training and sailed from Gravesend on 12th October, 1858, on the *Octavia* bound for Calcutta and then Meerut, the scene of the Indian Mutiny which had broken-out in 1857 and was not finally quelled until 1859. Both Major Turle and Major Carlisle had been in action putting down the Mutiny. Meerut is near Delhi and would have involved a very long overland journey from the east coast of India, following the valley of the Ganges for much of the way.

The Army Riding School at Maidstone, a central establishment, was a staging post for the colonies and in the 1860s as many as six hundred men would be stationed there. There were two barracks in the town, the first built in 1797 in response to the threat posed by Napoleon and which became home to the

West Kent regiment, and by 1813 the barracks on Sandling Road were used to train the cavalry's young horses. Twenty years later it became the Army Riding School and in October 1852, Captain Louis Edward Nolan (1818-1854) was given command of regimental troop training. In 1844 he had been appointed regimental riding master. Nolan was killed in action during the charge of the Light Brigade on 25th October, 1854. He was ADC to Brigadier-General Airey and was sent to Turkey to buy horses. He landed at Varna in July 1854 with three hundred. Then in October he carried Airey's order to Lord Lucan and Lord Cardigan. Lord Lucan apparently detested Nolan and when he heard that he had been killed, he said: 'He met his deserts, a dog's death - and like a dog let him be buried in a ditch.'

The voyage to India on the *Octavia* could have taken as long as sixteen weeks. She was a wooden screw frigate or converted sailing frigate, described on the embarkation document as a freight ship, that had been launched on 18th August, 1849 (subsequently scrapped in 1876). The ship was reported as being in good order with 'Good and sufficient water' and provisions that were 'Ample and of good quality'.

When his regiment - which had the nicknames of 'the Carbs' or 'Tichborne's Own' - returned to England, Marryat was promoted to second lieutenant - this time by purchase - on 28th January, 1862. He was to resign as a lieutenant in 1865 when he sold his commission. (Another source suggested that he retired as a vice on 2nd February 1864.) He then made the long and exhausting voyage to Australia. Did he go voluntarily, perhaps to seek his fortune? Or was his departure for the colonies linked to his resignation from the army? Sadly this is another aspect of his life where a lack of records leaves researchers in the dark.

The Carabiniers (6th Dragoon Guards) was a cavalry

regiment of the British Army and was a forebear of the Royal Scots Dragoon Guards, Scotland's only cavalry regiment. The regiment was descended from the Ninth Horse which had been raised to quell Monmouth's rebellion of 1685. The first colonel of the Ninth Horse was Richard, second Viscount Lumley of Waterford. Soon afterwards Lumley petitioned the Queen Dowager to permit renaming the regiment the Queen Dowager's Horse. The request was granted. Then, in 1691, during King William's Irish Campaign, the regiment distinguished itself and, as a result, it was posted to London and renamed the King's Carabiniers. The regiment helped quell Bonnie Prince Charlie's rebellion of 1745 to 1746. As it was recruiting almost exclusively from Irish protestants, it was redesignated the Third Irish Horse but it continued to be known as the Carabiniers. A reapportionment of the army establishment in 1788 resulted in the designation 6th Dragoon Guards (the Carabiniers) that was to remain for the next 133 years. The regiment was to fight through the Napoleonic Wars including the Peninsular Campaign, the Crimean War, Boer War and the First World War.

The cavalry was probably the hardest working arm of the British Army but had always been noted for its style and dash. Joining a cavalry regiment offered a life of excitement and danger as well as much hard work and stress, particularly for anyone learning to ride at the Maidstone Riding Establishment. They were expensive regiments to train and maintain. A cornet was the lowliest of officers. 'During the Civil War much was heard of "cornets" to describe a formation of horse. The "cornet" was the standard which, like the mediaeval banner, distinguished each corps. It gradually came to be used to denote the three hundred men of a cavalry unit. From this it became a rank and a "cornet", like an infantry ensign, carried the regimental flag in battle.' Officers of the 6th Dragoon Guards wore red sashes which did not show the colour of blood when used as a bandage.

India provided the British cavalry with many opportunities for exercise, training and fighting. Men and horses were always expected to be fit and this was achieved through regular daily exercise. The sword was the cavalry officer's main weapon although Marryat was in the army at a time when the rifle and more efficient artillery pieces were being developed. (I was very interested to find out that an earlier version of the cavalry officer's sword - the 1796 light cavalry sabre - 'had decorated blades and fishskin grips, bound with wire'. Very suitable for someone who was to make such an impact on the world of fly fishing.) In India in 1826 the British cavalry had used lances in action for the first time for some two hundred years when taking Bhurtpore. The introduction of the lance was controversial at the time and meant that a whole range of new drills had to be taught and learnt.

Marryat and his regiment arrived in the country soon after the East India Company had been abolished and the British Crown had assumed the government of India (on 1st November, 1858). British cavalry regiments were uncommon in India before the Mutiny and as there were few foreign postings for cavalry regiments, those regiments that were sent to India were often there for a long time. It wasn't an easy life. The troops suffered extremes of weather from the blistering heat of summer (with little or no proper clothing or protection from it which resulted in multiple cases of sunstroke), to freezing winter temperatures in the hills and mountains of the North-West Frontier. Rain and floods in the monsoon season caused chaos, dysentery and cholera and disease killed more soldiers than did battles. In 1879 Marryat's regiment lost six men to a flash flood on the Bara river near Peshawar during bridge building operations.

In India the troops suffered extremes of weather from the blistering heat of summer and little or no proper clothing or protection from it resulting in multiple cases of sunstroke, to freezing winter temperatures in the hills and mountains of the North-West Frontier. Rain and floods in the monsoon season caused chaos, dysentery and cholera and disease killed more soldiers than did battles. However, there were benefits to this lifestyle too and the possibilities of fishing for mahseer, shooting, big game hunting and pig sticking would have suited the sporting young officer very well.

Marryat's sea passage to India would have been a good rehearsal for the even longer voyage to Australia which he was to make in 1865 after he had sold his commission.

The practice of selling and purchasing commissions was to be abolished in 1871. The system for selling a commission was that the officer concerned had to offer his commission to the most senior officer of the rank just below his own. If that officer was unable or did not wish to buy the rank, then it would be offered to the next most senior officer. There were also regulations to determine how long an officer must serve in a particular rank before he could he purchase a promotion.

Although life in Australia was relatively primitive, it must have been very pleasant in comparison to much of his time in India.

4

Adventures in Australia

In about 1865, after his departure from the army, Marryat went to Australia, where 'he experienced the extremes of ups and downs' for about four years, some of which he spent doing a bit of 'squattering' (drifting around from place to place) on the Murrumbidgee river. Whether or not his departure was voluntary or forced upon him is only hinted at in William Senior's lengthy reminiscences of Marryat in the *Fishing Gazette*. Senior writing about the 'ambrosial nights we had in the homely millhouse after untiring days with our rods!' observed that 'Many a time I have been kept to the armchair, when the bedroom candlestick should have been lighted, by his recollections of the days when he had to earn the best living he could by stock riding in the bush, as many another well-born gentleman has done. On his return to England, his days of difficulty, at least so far as living was concerned, were over.' Senior seems to have been the only person to mention that there were 'difficulties' in Marryat's otherwise seemingly charmed life.

Marryat may have travelled to Australia on the SS *Great Britain* which sailed from Liverpool on 26th May, 1864, arriving in Melbourne in July, some sixty days later. A GT Marryat is recorded as a passenger on this ship but this could be a misreading of an original record or a typographic mistake. (Interestingly, the letter from Marryat published in *The Field* was credited to GTM and not GSM.) This was an age when time spent in the colonies was often seen as a panacea to the problems of sons with little or no prospects at home but there is no evidence that Marryat had any financial, personal or other problems. In fact there was a serious amount of money in his family and, after leaving the army, he never needed to work and was wealthy enough to employ large numbers of servants in later life, particularly when he moved to Salisbury.

Marryat arrived in Australia at a time when the population was growing rapidly and to maintain it required a 'continuous improvement in the production of commodities for overseas markets'. Also 'The decision of ambitious individuals . . . to try their luck in Australia' was accompanied by increases in investment as well as bringing to the country much needed new skills. Over a period of some three decades, these efforts brought great prosperity and Australians were to earn and spend more than the inhabitants of the UK, the USA or any other country in the second half of the nineteenth century. It was cheap to live in Australia where there were enormous opportunities and no need for a personal fortune. William Senior wrote that 'working bees are welcomed, and drones not required'. Melbourne was a gold rush town and 'in 1853 it was a community of weatherboards and canvas'. William Senior described it in the 1870s thus: 'Melbourne, alone of Australian capitals, may be measured by an old country standard without suffering by comparison. As it stands it is a grand city; criticised in the light of its history, it is wonderful. More than any other town, the capital of Victoria may be termed the colony itself.' And 'The fathers of Melbourne were wiser in their generation than those of Sydney and Brisbane. Like the founders of Adelaide, they planned their city well, insisting upon broad thoroughfares and plenty of open spaces, and jealously guarding them even when building allotments in the principal streets fetched three hundred pounds per foot.' Senior also noted that 'you may walk six miles diagonally across Melbourne, and at no time be more than a couple of hundred yards from some sort of garden, shrubbery, or reserve'.

The month before his departure an even more significant and important cargo, for fly fishermen at least, had made landfall in Australia. This followed various experiments and unsuccessful attempts that dated as far back as 1852, but more of that anon . . . It's worth, first, getting a feel for what Australia might have been like for the newly arrived Marryat and what might have drawn him there.

James Cook had sailed the length of the east coast of Australia and claimed it for the Crown in 1770 giving it the name of New South Wales. On 18th January, 1788, under the command of Arthur Phillip, what became known as the First Fleet, comprising officers, troops, civilian officials and convicts, landed on the north shore of Botany Bay. Phillip took formal possession of the new colony. As Stuart Macintyre wrote in his book *A Concise History of Australia*, soon 'The sound of an axe on wood, English steel on antipodean eucalypt, broke the silence of a primeval wilderness.' Early European navigators knew of the land that was to become Australia and had called it *Terra Australis Incognita*, a southern land beyond the limits of the then-known world, a place of mysterious and mythical beasts and wild animals, and fabulous wealth in the minds of those who had wanted to settle there for many years. The British authorities took possession of New South Wales under the doctrine that it belonged to nobody. Thus it was a better site for a colonial settlement than New Zealand as no treaty with its inhabitants or act of purchase was required. The aborigines that Cook saw were, he decided, few in number and nomadic inhabitants rather than owners of the land over which they travelled. The actual number of aborigines was a surprise to Phillip and his fellow settlers. They were 'confronted by a new social order in which autonomy of the individual prevailed and a form of political organisation based on impersonal regularity'.

The First Fleet consisted of eleven ships with 1066 people on board, thirty-one of whom died during the eight-month voyage, sailing via Tenerife, Rio de Janeiro and Cape Town. Over time, 23,600 women were deported, regardless of what crime they had committed, in a much needed attempt to balance the sexes in the new penal colony. More than seven hundred voyages were made in ships of between two and four hundred tons: they were a mix of square-riggers, barques and a few brigantines. Voyages took anything from seven to twelve months although one ship did reach Hobart in 104 days in 1834. Before 1810 more than one in ten convicts died on the journey and scurvy was a major killer prior to 1815 due to the lack of fresh vegetables. Five hundred and nineteen convicts lost their lives through shipwrecks in eighty years.

Although convict labour and the convict labour system were very inefficient, they were crucial to the development of what was to become New South Wales. The main arguments in favour of transporting criminals to Australia were probably the fear of crime in Britain, the demand for a terrifying deterrent and the provision of so-called free labour in the new colony. But convict slave labour was expensive and inefficient as the prisoners had to be forced to work which involved a lot of manpower and attendant high administrative costs. To build a stone bridge in Tasmania in the 1820s, using convicts, was more expensive than if free labour had been hired.

It was by accident, rather than by design, that Australia

became a land of opportunity. The consequences of shipping criminal and free settlers had unintended and unexpected consequences. Because of the shortage of labour, wages were higher in the infant Australia than in the UK. As a result, many convicts lived better there than they had or would have done in England. On arrival in Botany Bay, women prisoners were offered to commissioned officers, NCOs, privates and lastly convicts who had established themselves. Women not selected were taken ashore and assigned to huts and thence to work in factories. The process of assignment for work was a lottery and there were no proper barracks in Sydney for some years.

Many of the convicts were treated very badly and the floggings and other punishments, rather than having a beneficial effect, made many of the prisoners even more defiant and recalcitrant. Sir William Molesworth wrote: 'The two main characteristics of transportation are inefficiency in deterring crime and remarkable efficiency, not in reforming, but still further corrupting those who undergo the punishment. These qualities are inherent in the system.' Although transportation to Sydney had ceased by 1840 (although there was an abortive attempt to revive it in 1849-50), Sir George Grey, the second baronet and grandfather of Viscount Grey of Fallodon, told Parliament in 1850, when he was at the Home Office, that transportation was still essential as there were not enough prisons in Britain. Convicts were being transported at a time when Parliament and the authorities were using the death penalty as a punishment for ever more crimes and often seemingly petty ones by today's standards.

As with any new venture in a new country, the brave and adventurous could make their fortune. Land was cheap and more than plentiful although some capital was required to buy stock. Eager to rise to the challenge and make a fortune were army and naval officers who had been discharged after the

Napoleonic Wars and the younger sons of the landed gentry who would not inherit the family estate but who could establish themselves on the other side of the world. Wool was worth a lot of money and it would not deteriorate significantly on the long journey from the grasslands of Australia to the woollen mills of Yorkshire where it was converted to woollen clothing, blankets and carpets. By 1850, half of Britain's wool imports were from Australia and sales of Australian wool were worth over £2 million a year. In 1850 there were said to be 13 million sheep in New South Wales and once the merino breed had been introduced the improved quality of the wool was to sustain Australia's prosperity and growth for a hundred years. Of course, there were hazards - drought, bush fires, disease and fluctuations in market demand. (A reduced demand for wool in England in the 1830s caused the bottom to drop out of the market and prices crashed.) Because of the insecurity of the market, lack of land ownership title and the need for a quick return on money invested, little time or effort was spent on improving efficiency or looking after the land. The sheep cropped the land bare and their hooves compacted the ground, discouraging the native grasses from regrowing. This caused soil erosion which started to pollute the rivers and streams. It was soon very easy to see where the white man and his stock had been.

The early years of settlement were a time of severe hardship as crops failed to grow on the thin soil of Sydney Cove and stock was lost, strayed or had to be eaten. Help did not arrive until 1791 when the third fleet arrived with fresh supplies. By the end of 1792 when Phillip returned to England there was a substantial acreage of land under crops at Parramatta, and vegetable and fruit gardens were flourishing. It was this area of fertile land that saved the early settlers from starvation and total disaster.

Sealing and whaling contributed more to the colony's economy until 1830 than did crops and produce grown on Australia's less than verdant acres which were better suited to grazing sheep and cattle than growing crops. The area of cultivated land in 1850 was less than 200,000 hectares but this was to be increased to over 2 million hectares by the end of the 1880s. So Marryat was in Australia at a time of rapid increase and spread of agriculture. At the same time, the original graziers, who were little better than squatters, were becoming landowners and started to fence their land and to provide irrigation for the grass from dams and boreholes. Improved grazing meant better sheep and higher quality fleeces which commanded good prices until the middle of the 1870s, particularly from the UK which, by the 1880s, was taking 10% of national production.

In the middle of the nineteenth century Australia moved from being a penal colony to free and self-governing dominions. Some 80,000 free settlers landed in NSW in the 1840s and over a million more emigrated between 1851 and 1888. The majority made the long voyage on sailing ships which took many months to reach Australia. The British government allowed New South Wales a partly elected legislative council and this concession was extended to South Australia, Tasmania and Victoria by 1851. In 1855 the British parliament enacted the constitutions of New South Wales, Victoria and Tasmania; Queensland was separated from new South Wales in 1859, with its own constitution.

At the time that Marryat left on his voyage, emigrants went on board ship in England unsure of just how long it would be before they were to arrive in Australia. Once at sea, the ships were subject to the vagaries of wind and weather. Fair weather and good winds would produce a fast and relatively easy passage, but prolonged spells of inclement weather, gales and even storms would result in a much longer passage, often accompanied by heavy loss of life (the reduced numbers being balanced by the birth of children on the voyage). Most emigrants would have travelled in steerage accommodation between the main deck and the cargo hold. Ship owners were quick to realise that there was money to be made transporting emigrants and they put in an extra deck above the hold and below the upper deck. Conditions must have been pretty grim, with water from the hold sloshing about or seeping through gaps in the ship's planks. Light and ventilation were provided only by hatches, when and if they were opened. These hatches were, of course, battened down during a storm to prevent a ship being flooded. No lights could be used during a storm because of the risk of fire. Only wealthy migrants could afford the cost of travelling in one of the few cabins available to passengers. Although the *Norfolk,* as we will see, made the journey in eighty-four days, the average journey time was around a hundred days and some voyages took as long as 131 days, over four and a half months.

For Marryat the long journey, amongst unlikely companions confined in a close space, would have been one of uneventful routine, enlivened by the ceremony of crossing the Line. All sailors who cross the Line (or Equator to give it its more usual designation) during a voyage must, according to seafaring tradition, undergo rites of passage and ritual initiation into 'The Solemn Mysteries of the Ancient Order of the Deep' - rites which are believed to date back to the Middle Ages. (Some sources suggest that current ceremonies may be derived from Viking traditions.) Sailors who had never crossed the Line were referred to as either 'pollywogs' or 'slimy wogs' and were subjected to the initiation rituals performed by members of the crew who had already crossed into King Neptune's kingdom. At times these rituals were said to be quite aggressive and painful. At the end of the ceremony the new initiates were known as 'trusty shellbacks'.

Marryat would have been used to very hot weather after his time in India and being a former cavalry officer would have been a competent horseman. Even so, the very long days he would have spent in the saddle as a stockman in the outback, with little food or drink, under the searing summer sun, would have taxed his strength and powers of endurance. But, in fact, he must have had a far more interesting and enjoyable time than the brief contemporary reports suggest.

Marryat's decision to go to Australia may not have been as unexpected as previous accounts might suggest: he had family connections there. Charles Marryat (1827-1906), a nephew of Frederick Marryat, was ordained as an Anglican clergyman in 1852 and served a curacy in Kent before sailing to Sydney as a ship's chaplain in 1852. In Australia he was chaplain to two penal colonies before going to Adelaide where he became assistant curate of Holy Trinity Church. By June 1868 he had been made rector of Christ Church, North Adelaide, and archdeacon of Adelaide. That appointment was not well received as it was made on the casting vote of the bishop who was his uncle.

One of Selwyn's cousins, Alice, who had arrived in the country some years earlier, attempted to hire the town hall from the St Kilda Municipal Council to give a lecture but her request was turned down. The lecture - on the life and adventures of Lola Montez - was advertised in *The Argus* newspaper (published in Melbourne) as taking place on Thursday 21st March, 1861, at Hawthorn, to the east of Melbourne. (Lola Montez was an Irish dancer and actress who became famous as a Spanish dancer, courtesan and mistress of King Ludwig I of Bavaria.) In June 1855, she departed for a tour of Australia to resume her career by entertaining miners during the gold-rush of the 1850s. It is claimed that she performed her erotic Spider Dance at the Theatre Royal in Melbourne in September.

The Argus of Friday 5th October, 1866, recorded Selwyn

Marryat's attendance at the return fancy dress ball 'given by the citizens of Melbourne to the mayor and Mrs Bayles, in acknowledgement of the splendid entertainment at which they presided on the 20th of last month, [which] will be one event long memorable in the social annals of the colony'. The ball was held in the 'old Exhibition-building, which has been the theatre of so many interesting events important in the history of Melbourne'.

Marryat was back at the Exhibition building thirteen months later when he attended the royal levée held on 26th November, 1867. This was held for the Duke of Edinburgh who was 'now fairly domiciled - if only for a few weeks - in our midst'. The report in *The Argus* described the custom of holding levées as something that was 'eminently British in its character' and 'suits our habits thoroughly'. Marryat attended a levée 'such a one as has never been seen in the colony before. All who desired to honour the Prince as we have honoured none who ever yet stood on Victorian shores, passed before him yesterday in thousands, and never before did so many people come together for a similar purpose in Australia'.

The Government Gazette, reported in *The Sydney Morning Herald* of Friday 19th April, 1867, that Marryat was one of a number of 'gentlemen' who had been appointed a 'magistrate of the colony' for Menindee, a small township on the Darling river.

Menindee is about one thousand miles to the north-west of Sydney where Burke and Wills established a base camp on their ill-fated expedition to the north in 1860. History suggest that the first Europeans in the area in 1835, a party led by Major Thomas Mitchell, got off to a bad start with the local aborigines. It was not until 1852 that the first settler and effective founder of Menindee, Tom Pain, arrived with his family, to establish a home and business on the river. A Captain Francis

Cadell pioneered the operation of river steamers along the Murray and established a store in 1856. Once the news that the Darling river was navigable became known, settlers began to pour into the area. The 1860s were a period of rapid expansion for the town, which combined with the bad relations with the indigenous population, must have given Marryat plenty of work as a magistrate.

The fact that he was prepared to be a magistrate in 'the colonies' begs the question of why he took no part in public life on his return to England. He was never, it would seem, short of money and all his time was his own. He was educated, travelled and had served his country in India.

* * *

Now let's go back to that significant cargo that landed in Australia in 1864 . . . On 15th April of that year the *Norfolk* entered Port Phillip Heads and docked at the Railway Pier the next day, Saturday. In her cargo were some three thousand viable brown trout ova, the first ever to reach Australia and, as it turned out, the only successful shipment of trout ova to Australia.

The *Norfolk* operated a service from London to Sydney for Money Wigram & Co. The momentous voyage that saw the arrival of the first viable trout ova lasted eighty-four days. The *Norfolk* had set sail on the morning of 21st January, 1864. The man responsible for the first failed attempts and later the one and only successful attempt to ship trout eggs to Australia was Sir James Arndell Youl, described in the *Australian Dictionary of Biography* (online edition) as a pastoralist. Sir James was born in Parramatta on 28th December, 1811, and lived to the great age of ninety-three. He grew up in Tasmania and was educated in England. Youl and his wife left Tasmania for England in 1854 and set up home in Clapham Park,

Surrey, where he 'undertook many services for the colony over some fifty years'. He died in Clapham of senile decay and bronchitis on 5th June, 1904.

Although the desire of many English émigrés to Australia was to introduce English birds and mammals, often to satisfy a desire for recognised sporting quarry in their new homelands, the acclimatisation movement was international and new species were sent from the new colonies to England and Europe. In 1854 *La Sociéte Impérial d'Acclimatisation* was established in Paris, to be followed by an Acclimatisation Society of Great Britain and acclimatisation societies in most Australian colonies and local regions in Victoria and New Zealand. In Victoria, acclimatisation had its formal beginning at a meeting convened in St Patrick's Hall, Melbourne, on 6th October, 1857. The initial proposal was to start an ornithological society but this was extended straight away to a zoological society. It is also worth bearing in mind that the 'modern' science of piscicul-ture, the artificial rearing of fish (once carried out by the Romans and Chinese) had only been practised in Europe since about 1840. So a new science was going to be used to achieve what seemed to many at the time something that could not be achieved. The first fish hatchery had been established by the French government in Huningue, near to springs feeding the Rhine. Soon hatcheries were built in England, Scotland and Ireland, primarily in an endeavour to boost declining stocks of salmon.

A key member of the Victorian Zoological Society was an Englishman, Edward Wilson, who was born in London in 1811 and emigrated first to Sydney, in 1841, and then to Melbourne. Wilson spent some time as a grazier and then in 1848 he bought the newspaper *The Argus* which he ran most success-fully until 1857 when failing eyesight forced his retirement from journalism and publishing. He spent time in England, travelled widely and became a passionate advocate of acclimatisation. He wanted to export the wombat to England where he felt sure that it would be well received as 'a domestic animal not too large when killed to be consumed by a middle class family'. It was during his days in London that Wilson became actively involved in introducing salmon to Australia. On his return to Australia the Zoological Society was reinvigorated by him as the Acclimatisation Society of Victoria. Wilson became its first president in September, 1861. He had to retire from this position in the middle of 1864 when his still failing eyesight necessitated his return to England for an eye operation. That year he received a gold medal from the Imperial Acclimatisation Society of France and a silver medal from the Acclimatisation Society of Victoria.

It soon became evident that any attempt to introduce salmon to Australia would necessitate the shipping of salmon eggs (fry or fish would not survive the long journey or the high temperatures of the tropics and resulting lack of oxygen in the tank water). The first record of thoughts of introducing salmon to Australia dates to 1841 when Captain Chalmers, master of a ship trading between Tasmania and London, contacted Dr Mackenzie of Kinella, near Dingwall, to ask him to supply some salmon fry. The fry were not obtained but Dr Mackenzie suggested that it might be better to try transporting fertilised ova - a far-sighted recommendation. The first attempt to ship salmon ova to Australia in 1852 failed because it proved impossible to keep the eggs alive for the duration of the voyage. In his account of the experiment to the by now Royal Acclimatisation Society, James Burnett of the Tasmanian Survey Department, made the first suggestion of the need to use ice to control the temperature of the water. In February, 1858, Morton Allport, a salmon commissioner, recommended that for future efforts the ova temperature should be controlled by ice and that hatchery ponds be constructed to receive any viable ova that arrived in Tasmania.

The man whose work and practical experiments were to result in the successful export of ova to Australia now comes on the scene. Sir James Youl was helped in his work by other Australians then in London including Edward Wilson, a group which was known as the Australian Association. This group's first efforts were on the American clipper the *Sarah Curling* in 1860 when thirty thousand salmon ova were placed in a suspended gravel trough (in an attempt to isolate it from the ship's movement) which was fed with water cooled by passing it through an ice house containing fifteen tons of ice. The *Sarah Curling* left Liverpool on 25th February but on her fifty-ninth day at sea the last of the ice melted and the eggs died. Youl was now very anxious to find a ship sailing direct to Tasmania and a small iron steamer, the *Beautiful Star* was chosen, although she set out under sail to reduce the effects of the vibration of the steam engine and propeller on the ova. Again the ova were placed in trays on beds of gravel and complex methods installed to counteract the rolling and pitching of the ship, but with little or no success due to the lack of space. This voyage was beset with difficulties from the start and once again the ice did not last for the duration of what became an extended voyage. The last of the ova died on 17th May, when the ice had melted, although William Ramsbottom, who was in charge of the valuable cargo, had gone into the ice house on the 8th and found there a small box of ova packed in moss which had been placed there by James Youl. Some were still alive and did, in fact, hatch. This was a crucial observation that was to lead to the method used for the first successful shipment. Packing ova in moss had been used successfully in France when eggs from Huningue were despatched around that country. A Mr Brady, secretary to the Fisheries Board of Ireland, had also recommended the use of moss and had sent Youl 'a sketch showing a box with ova packed in layers of moss and fed from a tank of iced water', attached to a letter of 24th December, 1861. It was now obviously essential to success that the ova be delayed from hatching for as long as possible. Although another attempt had failed, the commissioners in Tasmania were still hopeful and William Ramsbottom was asked to return to England to assist in a new trial. Responsibility was delegated to Youl and the Australian Association in London. Edward Wilson and the Acclimatisation Society promoted the project to the Victorian government and were rewarded with a contribution of £500 towards the *Beautiful Star* experiment and a second £500 for the next trials. The Acclimatisation Society of Victoria was also donated £200.

Youl carried out experiments using moss in ice vaults belonging to the Wenham Lake Ice Company, London. Frank Buckland wrote in *The Field*: 'On Saturday, the 17th January, 1863, James A. Youl, Esq., Mr Robert Ramsbottom, of Clitheroe, Mr William Ramsbottom, and Mr Thomas Johnson, were engaged during the greater portion of the day in arranging the beginning of several experiments of a somewhat novel character.' Youl had five thousand salmon ova for his experiments and he packed small quantities in perforated wooden boxes containing a mixture of moss, charcoal and ice. 'Some of these boxes were placed in the ice vaults covered with blocks of ice, some two feet thick, and then buried under sawdust. Others were placed in a large ice box at the Wenham Lake Ice Company's office in the Strand [London], where [the] ice was kept replenished so that the melted ice water passed through the holes in the boxes.' The boxes were inspected forty-five days later and again after sixty-eight days. Both inspections showed the eggs to still be in good health and some were taken by Buckland and Johnson for hatching. Also on 25th March, the sixty-eighth day, one of the boxes in the vault was inspected.

Buckland was to write: 'I cannot describe the anxiety of all present to get a first sight of these ova, or the pleasure visible on every countenance to find as the moss was removed, our little friends alive and perfectly healthy.' Some of these were removed and they started hatching on 14th April and Buckland was able to report 'that the young alevins were strong and lively'.

The next time the ova were inspected was on 17th April, after ninety days. Most eggs were still viable and had hatched by 6th May. Some boxes were left for one hundred and twenty days when they were examined by Youl, Buckland and Edward Wilson. The ova were progressing towards hatching and even the moss was still alive. Youl realised that 'the best results were from a box . . . with blocks of ice (renewed as they melted) piled upon it, the water being allowed to percolate through it'. The conclusion of these experiments was that neither light nor running water was necessary, that ova could be kept healthy for more than one hundred days, and that growing moss with the roots attached was a suitable bed for them. Later, the Tasmanian Commissioners reported: 'The result of these experiments constitutes one of the most valuable discoveries yet made in the art of pisciculture, and must ever indicate an important era in its history.' Youl was to conclude that 'It appears that the best way next year is to place ova direct in an ice house'.

And so in 1864 the *Norfolk* was to sail with a cargo of salmon and trout ova packed in moss in the ship's ice house. Ninety days later living trout ova were delivered to trout hatcheries on the river Plenty in Tasmania, which Youl had visited in 1860. The *Norfolk* was a three masted, fully-rigged clipper ship of 953 tons, scheduled to sail to Melbourne (not direct to Tasmania) on 20th January. Money, Wigram and Co. agreed to donate, free of charge, fifty tons of measured space in the hold of what was one of its best and fastest ships. An ice house, capable of holding over twenty-five tons of ice was built amidships where the ship's movements would be felt least. Youl had planned to receive ova from the Ribble, through Robert Ramsbottom, but the fish had spawned already. He then asked Ramsbottom if he could source some ova from the Dovey in North Wales and, with the help of another pisciculturalist, from the river Tyne. He also appealed for help in a letter to *The Times* which was published on 6th January. So time was very short to find suitable sources of supply and to get the eggs to the London docks ready to be packed in the ice house. Youl was of the opinion at the time that this voyage was the only chance that he might have of getting 'this noble fish', the salmon, to Australia in a 'roomy, fast sailing, first-class ship'.

No ova were available up to 14th January and with only a week to go Youl must have been in despair. Nature was conspiring against him as he felt that the very frosty weather was discouraging fish from leaving the sea. A sudden change in the weather saw rivers full of fish ready to spawn and fishermen started to arrive in London with plenty of fresh ova 'as early as 5.0 am on Monday, 18th January'. Only two days to go. Youl's dramatic appeal had the desired effect and soon 40,000 ova were received from the Severn and an angler caught a 12lb cock fish on the Dovey and then succeeded in landing a hen fish. The fish were stripped into a bucket before being returned to the river. Space had been made available in an adjacent warehouse by the East India Dock Company where the eggs were packed in moss while ice was delivered into the ice house. All this work took time and was completed only thanks to Money Wigram delaying the ship's sailing for twenty-four hours. Building and filling the ice house must have been cold and hard work but at least the cold weather would have helped keep the ice well frozen. In fact the last block of ice was not loaded until 4 o'clock on the Wednesday afternoon and the ship sailed on the following morning, 21st January, with William

Ramsbottom on board to care for the precious cargo of approximately 90,000 ova packed into 164 boxes. But where were the trout ova?

Those who produced fertile trout ova also cut it very fine in delivering their precious contributions for the ice house. Although the prime objective was to send salmon ova to Tasmania, Morton Allport was very keen that some trout ova be included in the shipment, even if they had to be bought. Youl was not happy about the idea of including trout eggs because, as he wrote in a letter to *The Field*, of 12th November, 1864, 'I have made up my mind not to send trout ova with the salmon, because I believed that as trout grew faster, and arrived at maturity sooner . . . they would gobble up my little salmon'. Fortunately for trout anglers, two men, probably unaware of Youl's reservations, went ahead and produced the eggs. They were Frank Buckland and Francis Francis who had followed Youl's experiments in 1863 with great interest.

Buckland's ova were a present donated by Admiral Sir Henry Keppel from his stretch of the Itchen which ran through his garden at Bishopstoke near Winchester. Buckland was able to obtain nearly 1,500 ova from one pair of fish. He wrote: 'I recollect perfectly well that I found great difficulty in getting the trout from which these eggs were taken, having to wade right across the river, pulling a very heavy net behind me and getting thoroughly wet into the bargain.' Not much fun during a very cold spell of weather. Buckland arrived in London with his ova on Friday, 15th January which presented Youl with an immediate problem. Should he go against his instinct not to include trout ova, or accept them with good grace? Fortunately for Buckland and the development of fly fishing in Australia and subsequently New Zealand, Youl took the eggs and placed them at the bottom of the ice house, 'in the hope, however, that they would keep them in Melbourne'. Buckland was reported to have commented that Youl was in a mind to pitch them into the filthy water of the docks.

What of Francis Francis and his desire to contribute ova to the cargo? He came up with 800 ova on Monday, 18th January and a further 700 on the afternoon of Wednesday, 20th January, just hours before the *Norfolk* would sail. Francis's ova came, interestingly, from two tributaries of the Thames, rivers which today's trout fishermen would be unlikely to consider fishing let alone having ever held stocks of quality brown trout. Francis wrote to Youl later and stated: 'The ova sent is the finest trout ova I ever saw, and was taken from an 8 to 10lb fish which had all but finished spawning.' This fish came from Mr Spicer's mill at Alton on the river Wey. The second source of trout ova was the stream at High Wycombe, then known as the Wick but as the Wye in later years. Although the Wick was only a small stream, it produced surprisingly large trout - fish of four or five pounds in weight were common and some went as heavy as ten pounds, a leviathan for an English brown trout. Some of the early trout caught in Tasmania were of tremendous size and may well have come from those Wick ova. Some years later in a letter to *The Field* of 13th September, 1879, Francis described the Wick fish as being more like salmon than brown trout, brilliantly silver in colour 'they were very short and thick in make, and weighed heavier for their length than almost any fish I know'. The Wey also produced fish of high average weights.

Although, as we know, Youl had not planned to include trout eggs, he was fulsome and generous with his praise of the con-tribution made by Buckland and Francis. In *The Field* of 12th November, 1864, he was to write: 'If ever the disciples of Izaak Walton should have the pleasure of catching trout in Tasmania . . . they will be entirely indebted to these two gentlemen . . . and most unquestionably, if I had sufficient influence with the authorities, both these gentlemen . . . might be induced during the vacation to try their hand with a fly at the antipodes.'

While the *Norfolk* was at sea, Youl continued with his experiments at the Wenham Lake Ice Company and Buckland took some eggs which had been in store for ninety-three days and hatched them successfully in his hatching trough at the Royal Horticultural Gardens, South Kensington. They hatched into healthy little fish. All this time everyone was very anxious for news of the progress of the *Norfolk* sailing to Australia.

James Youl had arranged for the shipment on the *Norfolk* to be received by Edward Wilson in Melbourne. He was to be responsible for all the arrangements to transfer the eggs from the *Norfolk* to Tasmania. He had made arrangements with the Victoria Ice Company for a supply of ice and had secured the services of Her Majesty's colonial steam sloop, the *Victoria,* to convey the fragile cargo to Hobart Town. This ship was the colony's only warship and she had been built in England specially for the service of a British colony. Although she was a steamship she had sails and she sailed to Tasmania to reduce the risk of vibration upsetting the cargo of eggs. Wilson had even made a special trip round the bay to check on her motion and levels of vibration. The fact that such a ship was made available is indicative of the importance attached to these acclimatisation attempts by the government of Victoria.

The *Norfolk* tied-up alongside the Railway Pier on the morning of Saturday, 16th April. One of the boxes of eggs was opened by William Ramsbottom and Edward Wilson, in the presence of other members of the Acclimatisation Society of Victoria. It must have been quite a moment as the box was opened as there was no certainty as to what it would contain. As the moss was unfolded, it became apparent that 'about eighty per cent of the ova appeared healthy'. And surprisingly little of the ice had melted. Work continued all day, until dark, transferring the boxes of eggs into their temporary home in 'large, open wooden cases, provided by the Acclimatisation Society, and located in the forward part of the ship's lower hold'. Work on the trans-shipment was completed the next day and the *Victoria* was able to set sail just after lunch, with the trout ova on board although Youl and the Acclimatisation Society had intended that they remain in Melbourne. It seems likely that William Ramsbottom persuaded Wilson to send the trout ova to Tasmania. The ship arrived in Hobart on 20th April and her cargo was transferred once again, this time on to a barge which was then towed upstream to New Norfolk, arriving late that night. The next morning the barge was towed to the Falls on the Derwent where the cargo was unpacked from the remaining ice. The wooden boxes were unloaded and then slung on poles and carried by porters to the awaiting hatchery. The remaining ice was also taken to the hatchery and used to cool the water feeding the hatching ponds.

Work to unpack the fry started late in the afternoon and although it was carried on by candlelight, it was not completed until Friday night. 'The percentage of living ova varied greatly between boxes, but finally William Ramsbottom estimated that there were about 35,000 healthy salmon ova and some 300 trout ova, the latter being in a separate gravel bed.' The eggs were watched over with great care and dead or infertile ova were thrown out. Once the semi-dormant eggs were free of ice and in warmer water, the hatching process was speeded up. The sense of anticipation waiting for the first eggs to turn into yolk sac fry must have been intense. Jack Ritchie, in his very interesting book *The Australian Trout*, recorded that the trout started to hatch on 4th May, 1864, the salmon began hatching the next day and continued until 25th May for the trout and 8th June for the salmon. Of the roughly three hundred trout fry that resulted, thirty-eight were released into the river Plenty in 1866 and 133 were stripped, the eggs fertilised and then the first fertile brown trout ova were sent to Victoria in September. Morton Allport reported what was the first ever spawning of brown trout in the wild in Tasmania in July, 1866. This involved five pairs of fish. These original introductions provided the stock fish for trout fisheries elsewhere in Australia and New Zealand. In July, 1868, a trout of 9½lb and 26 inches long was caught in the river Plenty and in March, 1871, a man 'killed twenty-five genuine trout there in one day's fishing which was considered a good basket'.

As this was the only successful attempt to ship trout ova to Australia (future shipments were of salmon ova) which owed its success to Youl's experiments, persistence and energy in arranging the shipment, all the trout in Australia are descendants of these first few trout that hatched from the ova that survived transhipment around the world. Brown trout reared in Tasmania were introduced into Victoria and then to New South Wales in 1888. The offspring that resulted from these stockings were distributed widely in Tasmania, Victoria and New South Wales but it was not until 1901 that trout were introduced successfully to South Australia. And it was to be even later, the 1930s, before they were introduced into Western Australia.

Sir James Youl was honoured for his work, for which he received no payment and did everything - including travel - at his own expense, and claimed no credit. New Zealand presented him with a silver cup in 1866 and he received the gold medal of *La Société d'Acclimitisation*. He was created CMG in 1874 and KCMG in 1891.

* * *

Although Marryat travelled to Australia in the year after the successful shipment of trout ova, he does not seem to have had

anything to do with it. Trout were not introduced into the
headwaters of the Murrumbidgee river until 1888 by John
G. Gale. We know that Marryat fished as a boy (probably at
Chewton Glen) and his life-long love affair with fly fishing
started on the river Frome in Dorset, when his family moved to
Mapperton House, and would have continued on the Itchen
while at school. So it is probable that he fished in Australia but
there are no records to prove this. If he did fish there it would
not have been for trout for, as we've seen, the first ova had only
just arrived.

Major Turle recounted how he had first met Marryat on his
return from Australia in, what he thought was about 1868. In
fact, it must have been at least 1869, or even the following year
as Marryat would not have docked in London until the late
autumn of 1869. He sailed from Victoria for London on the
Ethiopian in August 1869 and he and Turle met fishing the Old
Barge. It was now, on his return to England, that Marryat's dry-
fly fishing career really started to develop.

The Times of 9th November, 1869 reported from Plymouth:

The ship Ethiopian*, 838 tons, Captain W. Faulkner, belonging to
Messrs. G. Thompson, jun, and Co., of Aberdeen, has passed up
Channel for London. Her cargo consists of 2,500 bales of woll and
other colonial produce, 11,293oz gold, and 20,000 sovereigns. The
only passengers are Mr A. F. Fletcher and Mr G. S. Marryat. The*
Ethiopian *left Port Phillip Heads August 25, crossed the equator
in long. 32 W. October 14, passed the Western Islands October 28,
and arrived off the Lizard November 5 - 73 days from Port Phillip,
and having sailed 14,772 miles, being an average of 202.35 miles
per day. From New South Wales to the meridian of the Horn strong
winds from north-west prevailed, and from the Cape to the equator a succession of north-east winds. Having no south-east trades,
the* Ethiopian *was compelled to tack from Bahia to Pernambuco.*

Thence to the Western Islands pleasant north-east trades were experienced.

William Senior was another who made his way to Australia and also to New Zealand. He had been a journalist for seventeen years and in 1875 (six years after Marryat returned) he was appointed by the government of Queensland as its first *Hansard* editor. He was an expert shorthand writer who had been trained in the press gallery of the House of Commons, an accomplished journalist and a fine writer of quite a number of books. He had started his career in newspapers in Manchester in 1858. Although he spent two months in New Zealand, in 1878, most of the time was spent travelling and he managed to fish for only eight days on the Lee, not far from Outram near Dunedin.

Senior suffered from homesickness in Queensland but perhaps more importantly from trout sickness. In his book *Lines in Pleasant Places* he described a lone ride along a sandy track in the Australian bush 'flicking off a wattle blossom singled out from the yellow mass with my hunting crop, fancying it is a fly rod, and rehearsing the old trick of sending a fly into a particular leaf'. As he rode along he took the latest copy of the *Gentleman's Magazine* 'newly arrived by this morning's mail' and read through 'a "Red Spinner" article on 'Angling in Queensland' with an author's pardonable desire to see how it comes out in print'. His musing then took him back to a notable day on the Chess one June, when the fish failed to rise and his fishing was ruined by a man cutting his grass and emptying the cuttings into the river. Sport was very much better the next day when he caught some large, unattractive fish that he described as 'degenerates' and another thirty fish which averaged $3/4$ lb each.

Senior's trout sickness was cured by a visit to Tasmania -

which involved a journey of eight days - where he caught his first trout on the North Esk. He was one of a small number of people who saw the original trout hatchery in operation in Tasmania and the hatchery in New Zealand at Hagley Park, Christchurch. The ship on which he sailed from Sydney to Auckland was called the *Rotorua* and he went on to Tauranga on the *Taupo*. In Australia he also spent time on cattle and sheep stations and hunted and shot wild horses and opossums.

Summing up his visit to Tasmania in *Travel and Trout*, Senior was not prepared to say if trout had any moral nature but he feared that the Tasmanian trout 'is, by comparison with his ancestors in the old country, a degenerate individual'. He then wrote that in comparison to a trout from the Kennet, one from the Tasmanian Derwent 'shall be longer, broader, thicker, and vastly heavier than the other. But in all other forms of comparison the colonial must hide his head'. He was equally disparaging of locally-tied flies: 'mostly large and coarsely made'. And 'the casts that are sold to local fishermen are of the strongest character'. Fishing methods tended to be even more coarse and unsportsmanlike using large hooks, often trebles, with a substantial bunch of worms attached. This was said to be, in part, because 'During the best months of the season the streams are literally gorged with insects, larger, fatter, and no doubt more toothsome than the gauze-winged little sham creatures of the other side of the world. Naturally the trout are gorged too.' His less than fulsome praise for the fish that he caught may be a result of fishing during the middle of the season which was known to be the least favourable time to be on the water. Poaching was also a major problem.

5

Prince of Fly Fishers

'Field sports unified Victorian countrymen in common pleasures' although fishing was less fashionable than shooting or
hunting and, with the exception of trout and salmon rivers,
licences to fish were granted freely. This was at a time when
much of the value attached to Hampshire farms was in the
shooting and fishing rights. A second wave of real popularity in
shooting had started in the 1850s and lasted - unchecked but
influenced by political and social factors - until the start of the
First World War. The fluctuating fortunes of farming in the
nineteenth century were matched by a similar rise and fall in the
numbers convicted of poaching. Convictions rose when farming was suffering and incomes were low.

Colonel Peter Hawker, who served in the cavalry and fished
the Test many years before Marryat, was gazetted cornet to the
1st Royal Dragoons in 1801 and moved into the 15th Light
Dragoons two years later. He was a passionate wildfowler who
enjoyed all forms of shooting and fishing. Although fishing was
not his first sporting interest, he is known to have caught many
thousands of Test trout during his thirty-five years' fishing the

river. In spite of the fact that he caught vast numbers of fish, he was frequently less than complementary in his comments on the river and the quality of its fishing. For example, on 31st July, 1815, he 'Went over to Ponton's at Stockbridge. Found the fly fishing, as it almost always is at this celebrated though infamously bad place, not worth a penny. The cockney-like amusement of bobbing with a live mayfly is all that this miserable river does for; indeed, scarcely a fish ever moves till about the last quarter of an hour that you can see to throw a line.' At the end of August he claimed that the season had been the worst ever known and that he had caught but thirty-seven brace of trout with a fly 'which number I have, before now, exceeded in one day'.

He had bought 'the celebrated fishery of Mr Widmore' at Longparish and then on 23rd February, 1818, he bought Mr Sutton's lease 'with which it was encumbered, and became possessed in fee simple of one of the finest trout rivers in the world'. At the end of that year's entries, he noted: 'As the whole fishery which goes through our premises was purchased by me of Mr Widmore previous to this season, I never made a regular day's fishing, but merely went angling for a few hours before dinner, and seldom failed to kill a large dish of trout whenever we wanted them. I therefore have this year kept no account, though, were I to include nets and all, I should perhaps have noted down about a ton weight of trout, &c.; this is about half of what the previous occupier took in a season by dragging.'

Col. Hawker in his diary for 29th September, 1840, recorded: 'I went and killed 4 large trout that were wanted for dinner, the best of which was nearly 2lb. This must end angling, as the fish, I see, are beginning to spawn.'

In December of the same year he wrote that he 'Left Longparish, and went, for a change of air from the pestilential vapours of that low water-meadow country'.

At Longparish on 27th May, 1842, he 'went out for about an hour and a half with fly rod, and brought in 24 prime trout. Not being in an enemy's country [ie, poaching a neighbour's water], I left off when I might have caught, perhaps, as many more.' He wasn't averse to using poacher's methods, if necessary, as on 5th April, 1848, when he 'got 3 fine trout with a stick and wire'.

Writing on 20th May, 1853, he noted that: 'One of my fishery tenants, Mr Macleod, in the first week of March, had killed, in a severe winter's day, 15 brace with a fly, and he kindly sent me a few as red and good as salmon. This phenomenon is accounted for by the continued rains flooding all the low lands, and washing down constant winter food for the fish.' Later the same month: 'Another circumstance to record - Captain Duff and his friend came to my river to fish, and, in spite of the adverse weather, had a few days' good sport; and, what is a miracle, every trout was better in season (though in April) than, for these twenty years, I have seen them - even in June and July, the only time they have hitherto been fit to eat. They were quite red, firm, and full of curd - in short, delicious.' Sadly, he continued that his 'lamentable illness' had denied him from taking part in the best angling season on record.

Hawker was unusual for trout fishermen of his time in that he lived on the river and fished regularly throughout the season. This was at a time when most anglers who fished the Test and the other main chalkstreams in the middle decades of the nineteenth century visited the river perhaps only once or maybe twice in a season but when they did, they would stay for quite some time. These leisurely gentlemen anglers would appear on the river for the first time in April for the grannom hatch, again in May for the mayfly and were gone usually by the end of June. One or two might reappear in the autumn for a go at the grayling.

Major Turle also owned waters on the Test, at Newton Stacey.

C. Ernest Pain described how Turle 'held gatherings for the Mayfly festival', and it was at Newton Stacey that he first met Marryat and fished with Halford, Major Carlisle, A. N. Gilbey (one-time honorary secretary of the Houghton Club) and other well-known anglers. 'Long rows of trout were laid out each evening on the lawn at Newton Stacey, for this length of river was always well stocked and there was no limit in those happy days.'

As someone who was happy to resort to devious methods in pursuit of trout, Hawker would no doubt have appreciated a technique developed by Major Turle, that Halford recounted in his book, *Development of the Dry Fly*. On the Test at Newton Stacey there was a narrow, deep and slow-flowing stream known as the Black Ditch. Halfway down the Black Ditch there was a bridge over it. Fish in the Black Ditch were some of the biggest and hardest-fighting of Test trout but they rose only to spent gnats or sedges. Turle developed a very dubious way of catching them.

When Turle wanted to fish the Black Ditch he would send his keeper out, earlier in the day, 'to collect a great number of the imagines [imagos] of both sexes and keep them alive in a basket'. Come the evening, the keeper would be positioned with his basket of flies on the bridge over the ditch. Turle would position himself some way downstream. The keeper would take a fly from his basket, pinch its head 'to make it appear spent', and then drop it on to the water. He would carry on like this until some of the big fish started feeding on the artificial, man-made hatch of spent mayflies. Halford recalled that 'Turle would mark down most accurately the spot where the big fish were rising, and as soon as one came fairly on the feed, would put his artificial spent gnat once or twice over the trout'. Turle told Halford that he had caught some of his biggest fish employing this tactic.

Halford knew that fish in the Black Ditch would rise to the
spent gnat without needing any encouragement from what he
described as 'dodging' and he knew that Marryat loved the
place because it had been the scene of many fine battles in its
clear, pellucid waters. 'The fish were very difficult to rise, and
terrifying when hooked, and the great master himself told me
that on one June day many years ago he was utterly smashed up
by nine consecutive fish he hooked, all monsters, although he
was fishing with the stoutest and strongest gut he possessed.'
Halford did finish his account with a strong recommendation
that his readers should not be encouraged to try Turle's technique which he doubted could be termed fair fly fishing.

In *Dry-Fly Fishing*, Halford recounted another incident
involving Marryat and the spent gnat, also at Newton Stacey.
Halford used this story as an illustration of the importance of
leaving your fly on the water of a slow stream for as long as possible. Halford recalled that Marryat cast to a fish rising in an
almost stagnant bay of a small side stream. He had cast over a
plank which served as a bridge over the neck of the little bay. He
then waited for some minutes before his patience was rewarded
by a bold rise. Marryat set the hook and instructed the keeper
to remove the plank so that he could play the fish, 'a good one,
nearly 3lb'. Halford maintained that 'Not one in a hundred
anglers would have waited so long for the rise'. Marryat must
have had an interesting few moments as the keeper removed
the plank, with the attendant risk that his sudden presence and
actions might scare the fish.

Marryat, and Halford perhaps even more so, was often very
happy to sit and observe or wander over the waterside meadows,
rather than spend all day fishing. In a letter to H. S. Hall, July,
1883, he wrote that on the 11th of the month he had 'yarned
and carried the net' when fishing Wickham's water, which he
also fished on the 8th and the 12th. A bit further on, he wrote

'I went to Somersetshire and pooped about on two-foot streams and yarned'. Halford quoted Marryat as saying to him that 'a day at the river side watching a first-rate performer was quite as enjoyable as one passed in solitude fishing oneself'. One July day three years later, in 1886, Marryat and Halford were 'wandering rather than fishing in the middle of a hot calm afternoon' when they noticed a fish rising to a small insect. This happened a number of times 'over an area of perhaps two or three square yards'. They thought that the rises were too deliberate for a smutting or bulging fish but they did not think that the fish was taking duns or spinners of which there were very few to be seen on the surface of the river. Action was now required to solve the mystery of what the trout was feeding on. 'A cinnamon quill on a 000 hook tempted the fish - a good one nearly 2 lb - at the first cast.' The two set to work immediately to carry out an autopsy on the fish. The undigested food consisted of between thirty and forty specimens of the same species. 'Fortunately, Mr Marryat knew the insect at once as the Corixae, a small water-beetle about a quarter of an inch in length'. Halford had never before seen one in any of his previous autopsies and he recorded that it was not until the summer of 1887 that he discovered another one in a trout of about three pounds, 'caught in the same part of the shallow'.

As good an angler as Marryat was, he, like every other trout fisherman, had his less successful days. One such experience with Halford gave rise to a now-defunct expression 'being Kimbridged'. Sanctuary was to write a poem on the subject which was published in the *Fishing Gazette* in May, 1924, and based on losing a very large fish the previous year. In a footnote to the poem Sanctuary wrote: 'It frequently happened that after playing a good fish for some few minutes, the fly would come back uninjured. Halford attributed this to the hook point catching on a scale, as he once found a scale when the fly returned.' On the day in question, 'a lovely day, with a light north-west wind', the hatch of mayfly was notable for its duration rather than sheer number of flies. Both Marryat and Halford found that the fish would rise to and take 'any of the small Mayflies on No. 2 hooks, or such flies as the Welshman's Button, Hammond's Adopted, Artful Dodger, or Kimbridge Sedge, seemed equally tempting'. While every fish covered would rise and take the proffered fly, once the angler had set the hook and the fish 'went away with that typical dash of a Mayfly trout', as soon as it was checked and turned, the line went slack and told 'the unfortunate fisherman that it was free'. 'Striking more slowly, or more quickly, holding the hooked fish as much as possible, or letting it run freely, every conceivable plan was tried and tried in vain. Throughout the day we both agreed that at least three out of four hooked fish got away.' This was not an entirely new experience for Marryat although he had never suffered to such an extent as on that day and Halford said that 'for ever after he spoke of it as being "Kimbridged" '. In spite of both men losing so many fish, they ended up with a bag of nine brace (four and a half each) although the average weight was less than the average for a good mayfly day at Kimbridge. The next day Halford fished at Houghton where he was Kimbridged by four out of six trout that he rose and hooked in succession during a heavy hatch of fly.

Late in 1899 when reminiscing about his life and times with Marryat, Halford recalled:

Mr Marryat insisted that a dry-fly fisherman must be equipped with rod and line with which he could with ease cast against anything short of a hurricane. His experiments indicated the necessity of the rod being distinctly stiffer and the line heavier than those then in use; he also advocated a short taper to the line.

The split cane rod was spoken of and occasionally seen in this country, but the majority of our English fly fishermen dubbed it a transient American fad. The late Mr Deller was making the first of his glued-up rods, and even these showed the same excellent qualities of action and balance so marked in all the rods manufactured by his firm up to the day of his death. In 1880 he made me my first split cane rod; it was eleven feet nine inches long, slightly stiffer all over and heavier in the point than the rods then in vogue. Subsequently it was gradually cut down to stiffen it, and eventually made a serviceable eleven feet rod. It was too heavy for me, but my good friend Marryat accepted it and used it for many years.

This may well have been the rod that Halford referred to when he wrote: 'my late friend Marryat, who was *facile princeps* in long single-handed casts, on calm days often achieved the extraordinary feat of casting thirty yards with an eleven-feet rod.' (Deller had a fishing tackle shop, Eaton and Deller, at 6 and 7 Crooked Lane, London EC.)

* * *

For someone who was so passionate about his fishing it seems strange that Marryat never owned any water himself and was involved in the formation of only one fishery, the one on the upper Kennet, at Ramsbury, formed by Halford and three others. But Marryat and Francis Francis did rent a stretch of the Itchen, at Winnal, above Winchester, from 1879 to 1882, although he was to write to H. S. Hall in 1883 referring to the water in the present tense, no doubt because he continued to fish there when the lease changed hands. When he was living in Salisbury he rented some fishing on the Avon. In his obituary of Marryat, William Senior wrote: 'Naturally with his fame and popularity he had the run of the choicest streams' and he certainly was never without an invitation to fish either the Test or Itchen and some other rivers in the UK. There seem to be no suggestion anywhere that he ever fished abroad as, for example, Skues did in Bosnia in 1897.

When Marryat and Francis took on the fishing on the Itchen, it was in a very neglected state. It was described as being infested with pike and almost without any trout. This was the same water that was leased by Irwin Cox, one of the proprietors of *The Field*, from 1883 until 1919. Skues wrote how the pike and big cannibal trout were netted and removed by Francis and Marryat and the river stocked with trout which he thought probably accounted for the good head of fish he saw when he first fished there in 1883. During Marryat's tenancy John Locke was the river keeper. In a letter to H. S. Hall, postmarked 11th July, 1883, Marryat wrote: 'Our Water is very much improved I think - I should expect to kill 3 brace of nice fish any decent day.' It seems to be one of only two times that Marryat had what one might describe as his own fishing, the second being two lengths of the Avon that he rented with Tom Sanctuary. Today the Itchen fishery is better known as Abbotts Barton. It was at Abbotts Barton that Skues fished for nearly fifty years and developed his nymph fishing techniques and flies.

When Marryat moved to Salisbury he and Sanctuary rented three or four miles of the Avon along with the shooting rights and 'had good times together on the Nadder, Wyly [*sic*], and Bourne - three affluents of the former river'. Francis Francis went to stay and fish on occasions with Marryat and Sanctuary, as did Halford. Marryat was also a frequent guest on the Kennet and fished public waters including Old Barge which he had fished first as a schoolboy. Sanctuary used to stay with Marryat when he was living at Shedfield to fish the Test with him. They also had many 'long, delightful days' at Houghton, Kimbridge and Newton Stacey, all on the Test.

It was a cold day, with a north-east wind, spent fishing for grayling on the Test at Houghton, on 21st October, 1881, that was to provide the cognomen which Halford and other friends often used when talking about Marryat, 'poor duffer'. Halford failed to catch a single sizeable fish and recorded the fact in his fishing diary. Marryat was fishing another part of the same water and when they met at the end of the day, Halford asked him to record his day in his diary. Halford was to write: 'His [Marryat's] entry reads thus: "Poor duffer G. S. M. had 6 (1³/₄, 1¹/₂, 1¹/₄, 1¹/₄, ³/₄, ³/₄ lb.); took anything chucked, any-how - Geo. S. Marryat. P.S. - Returned 9 besides." I give this *in extenso*, as eminently characteristic of the man, and because ever after, among ourselves we often styled him by his own cognomen "poor duffer".'

Halford described in his autobiography how Marryat had fished a length of the Frome, many miles from Dorchester, in what he termed, rather interestingly, the 'olden days'. He described the river as starting off flowing through a park under an avenue of trees, then through a series of open shallows with many twists and turns and some deeper pieces of water. Halford was to fish the Frome in 1898 and the following year. Halford's use of the phrase 'olden days' rather suggests that this was before the enlightenment of Halford's dry-fly purism had been visited upon Marryat. Sanctuary's remark that Marryat did not learn to fish the dry fly until his return from Australia would sup-port this contention. Sanctuary was able to date the start of Marryat's dry-fly fishing - as opposed to fishing with wet flies or spinning with minnows - to his return from Australia. According to Sanctuary he learnt how to fish a dry fly from John Hammond, who had taught him, Sanctuary, when he was at Winchester College. The inference to be drawn from this statement is that Marryat must have fished the wet fly while he was a pupil. Sanctuary maintained that Marryat was quick to see the 'applicability to southern waters' of the dry fly 'and there is no doubt that he was more instrumental in bringing it to its

Marryat - from the Fishing Gazette.
Photographer: Messrs Witcomb & Son,
10 Catherine Street, Salisbury.

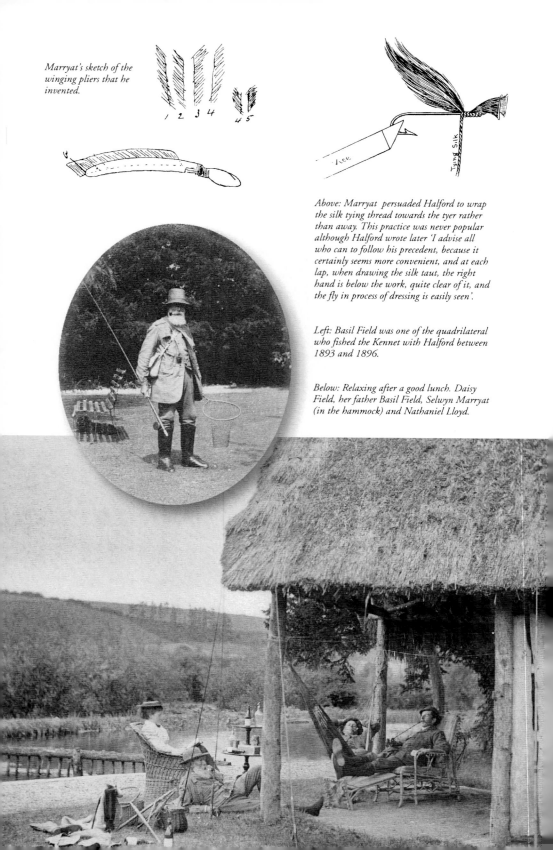

Marryat's sketch of the winging pliers that he invented.

Above: Marryat persuaded Halford to wrap the silk tying thread towards the tyer rather than away. This practice was never popular although Halford wrote later 'I advise all who can to follow his precedent, because it certainly seems more convenient, and at each lap, when drawing the silk taut, the right hand is below the work, quite clear of it, and the fly in process of dressing is easily seen'.

Left: Basil Field was one of the quadrilateral who fished the Kennet with Halford between 1893 and 1896.

Below: Relaxing after a good lunch. Daisy Field, her father Basil Field, Selwyn Marryat (in the hammock) and Nathaniel Lloyd.

QUILL BODIES FOR FLIES.

It may be advisable, for the benefit of the enthusiasts in fly-fishing who still tie their own flies, to give a few hints on the material mentioned by Mr Francis, in his charming article in the Christmas number of The Field, as "quill." Let no one suppose for a minute that he can get it from his "grey goose quill," or any ordinary feather. It requires careful selection and careful dyeing to arrive at a satisfactory result. It is obtained from the tail feather of the peacock; a single herl is divested of the metallic fur which adheres to it by repeatedly drawing the strand sharply downwards, from the point to the heel, between the ball of the forefinger and the thumb nail of the right hand, the end of the strand being held in the left hand. The strands from the eye of the peacock's feather are those selected; those from below the eye of the feather will be found to be of a uniform dark dun, and are of little use, as they are too dark to take the light olive-yellow or brown tints required for the bodies of the duns and spinners, for which alone they are useful. The strands from the eye of the feather are of a lighter dun (if obtained from a good feather, those with the largest eyes being the best), having one edge of much lighter colour than the other. It is this that gives the ribbed appearance to the body of the fly when tied, which constitutes its killing quality. I remember a fisherman on the Itchen telling me one day that he had killed with a particular quill gnat which he showed me, having this rib, while he could not do anything with any of the rest of the half-dozen which he bought with it, though they were otherwise exactly the same in hackle and wing. But to return to our quill. Having, as I said, selected a good feather, cut off the eye about half an inch below the metallic green; the rest is valueless for quill bodies. If, on stripping a strand, it shows nearly all the width a pale colour, you are right; if not, go higher up the eye. For grey quill gnat the natural colour is right, and with a light blue dun hackle, and light starling wing, it is a deadly fly on a bright day; the same with darker wing and hackle is better for a cloudy day. The quill dyed olive with onion dye, and a blue dun hackle dyed in the same dye in three shades and sizes, no fisherman should ever be without. I should not be afraid to back it against any other single fly that can be tied. For the brown dun mentioned by Mr Francis I use Judson's olive-brown, which looks purple when mixed with water, but, mirabile dictu! dyes olive-brown. This, with a ginger-brown hackle, and starling (or, for a change, coot) wing, is a killer for the autumn months. A fine red spinner is tied by using Judson's light red for the quill, with a coch-y-bonddu hackle and light dun hackle wings. This fly should be ribbed with very fine gold wire. Of course, these flies may be varied to any extent by dyeing to match any required shade. If a fly is required of a uniform colour, the quill should be so laid on that the light edge of the quill overlaps and hides the dark edge. This lightens the colour of the fly considerably, but does away with the ribbed look of the body. I think white peacock herl would make a good body dyed, but have been hitherto unable to procure any, though I have been promised some by several friends. The roots of some of the strands of the longest tail feathers of the peacock are sometimes nearly white for an inch or two from the base. I have used them for light brown duns with success. For all the dyes the feather should be soaked in hot alum mordant before attempting to dye them, and they should be well washed in cold water when the tint required is obtained, or the quill will rot. I do not agree with the theory of Ronald, that a fish spits out a hard-bodied fly of quill or hair quicker than a soft-bodied one of fur or dubbing. Any way, if he does, it is good enough for me if I can get him to take it into his mouth at all; and that takes some doing on parts of the Itchen and Test nowadays.

G. T. M.

Our correspondent is a past master in the art, as may easily be seen, and all his advice may be relied on. Can any correspondent oblige us with the eyes of a few tail feathers from a white peacock?—En?

Left:
Marryat's letter in
The Field, 8th January,
1881 on quill bodies
for flies was the first of
only two known published
pieces of Marryat's
writing.

Below:
Marryat's second letter,
this time to the Fishing
Gazette, 28th June,
1884, was on the subject
of who invented dry-fly
fishing.

WHO INVENTED DRY-FLY FISHING?

SIR,—I believe the late James Ogden, of Cheltenham, claimed to have been the inventor of the dry-fly system, but I expect it is a case of evolution, and that the first man who threw a dry fly is lost to fame, caret quia vate sacro. I see your correspondent, "Hampshire," saw me cast twenty-eight yards of line with a single-handed rod; it was not measured, and if I were you I should reel in about six yards two feet eleven inches and threequarters, or you will raise "Merry Nell" at the forthcoming FISHING GAZETTE Tournament on July 26, unless I come and do it, or burst a little gut trying to do it. I have just been staying at Houghton Mill. I fished one evening at Piddlesworth, and got a brace of fish and two great silly dace that hadn't as much judgment as not to rise like grayling, and so met a dry death. I don't hanker after fishing a single blank in hay fields; docks is cusses, and thistles is blisphemy, and all fishermen's recording angels have to be double-balked in hay time. Who might "Hampshire" be, if it is not a breach of etiquette to say?—I am, &c.,

GEO. I. MARRYAT.

[We must leave "Hampshire" to make himself known to Mr. Marryat, if he cares to do so. We can fully sympathise with Mr. Marryat and the exasperating state casting from a hay field induces in all but angels. Last Monday we had a fair dose of this form of hay fever. You see a fish rise just on the edge of the weeds, say within an easy cast up stream, fifteen yards perhaps. You kneel down and creep as near the water as possible to get free of over-hanging green things. Two or three flutters of the fly to dry it, then a nice back cast, and with your eye intent on the feeding place, you make the forward cast. Everything goes nicely until you have got full steam up, and then—bang—your fly has got round a slender but tough bit of rye grass, or the red scale-like flowers of the dock. On such an occasion the best thing to do is to set your teeth well into the screw of your whisky flask and take a solar observation, remember the "World's" advice as to what to say, and repeat "Godfrey Daniel's blast and furnace works" until relieved. Repeat it to the farmer if he asks you why you don't walk "all over the field."—ED.]

Mill on the Kennet.

Butcher's Corner.

The Long Bridge at Chilbolton.

'Our fishing box on the Kennet.'

Opposite and above: Marryat's own photographs from Halford's An Angler's Autobiography, 1906.

Below: Photograph by Charles Moss, captioned 'Farewell to Houghton', also from
An Angler's Autobiography. From left: Selwyn Marryat, William Senior, Nathaniel Lloyd and F. M. Halford.

Letter from Marryat accompanying his cheque in payment of the rent for Shedfield Grange.

March 26. 85

Dear Admiral Phillimore

Please find cheque for rent of The Grange to date viz:

Shed. a.   1 . 15 . 2 ⎱ Michas
Blackmansh. 1 . 9 . 1 ⎰ Cockrel
            ————
            3 . 4 . 3

½ y. rent 32 . 10 . 0
            3 . 4 . 3
          £ 29 . 5 . 9

Shedfield Grange
Botley

Novr 5 1884.

My dear Admiral Phillimore

I was in Salisbury today, and have taken the lease of a house in the Close there. I therefore write as a matter of form (though I believe Mrs Marryat has

Letter, 5th November, 1884 to Admiral Phillimore advising him that Marryat and his family were about to move to Salisbury.

Phillimore) to ask Captain Travers,
... who expressed a wish to ...
... know if we were leaving,
agreement, of my intention to ask him if he has
to leave the Grange - should any idea of coming
any friend of yours wish to back here again, and
take the grange, I would shall probably hear from
give it up short after him in the course of a
Christmas - I have written day or two

Yrs truly

W. S. Marryat

Marryat's will was drawn-up when he and his wife Lucy Dorothea were living in Edinburgh. It was proved and registered on 31st March, 1896. The gross value of his personal estate was £1474:6:0 and the net value £1375:9:10.

No. 20 The Close, Salisbury. Marryat and his family lived here from 1885 until his death on 14th February, 1896.

Marryat's memorial plaque in the Cloister Garth, Salisbury Cathedral.

There is also a small commemorative plaque in The Close dedicated to Eva Caroline Marryat who died on 28th April, 1943.

present stage of development than any fisherman who exists'.

Before Halford took on the tenancy of the Ramsbury fishery in 1893, Marryat carried out a thorough inspection of the upper Kennet waters on offer. It ran to a considerable length - about five miles - with one landlord who owned both banks and wanted to let it on a lease. Marryat described it to Halford as a 'typical stretch of dry-fly water requiring only liberal expenditure and judicious management to make it one of the best fisheries in the South of England'. Marryat suggested that they should form a syndicate but Halford and those who had business experience felt that a syndicate was too closely associated with business swindles and so, at Marryat's suggestion, it became known as a quadrilateral. The members of the quadrilateral with Halford were Basil Field, William Quiller Orchardson RA, and Nathaniel Lloyd. Marryat declined to join the quadrilateral probably, Tony Hayter suggested in his biography of Halford, because he did not have the wherewithal. I find this hard to accept as he maintained a large household employing a cook, governess, house maids, parlour maids and gardener and had private means. There was plenty of money in the Marryat family as is indicated by his uncle Frederick's substantial inheritances which, admittedly, he did manage to lose on more than one occasion. The annual rental for the fishing was £300 to which would have been added the costs of keepers, stocking and other costs of running a fishery. Whether or not Marryat's share would have been beyond his means cannot be determined. The only comment that hints at his financial status was that of William Senior: 'On his return to England [from Australia], his days of difficulty, at least so far as living was concerned, were over.' But when probate was granted on 31st March, 1896, his estate was valued at £1,474 6s 0d, something of a pittance compared to some of his very wealthy fishing friends such as Samuel Montagu and even Francis Francis who left over £3,000. The executors of his estate were his wife and his sister Agnes Charlotte's husband George Edward Eliot who was then a Justice of the Peace.

In 1890 the Hungerford Fly Fishing Club left the Kennet and moved to the Wylye, renaming themselves the Wilton Fly Fishing Club. They leased several stretches of the river, one of which they still hold today. It was the lease of the Wylye from Wilton to Stapleford that took the longest to agree. Henry Collins, the club's secretary, suggested bringing in Marryat to arbitrate. This was agreed and Collins immediately accepted Marryat's valuation and the lease was quickly concluded.

In 1892 the Wilton Club found it needed to call on the experience and knowledge of Marryat again. The club was having problems with a local clergyman whose parishioners had long fished the bottom of the river Till before it joins the Wylye at Stapleford and he acted as their champion in trying to claim some sort of traditional 'right'. This dispute dragged on and eventually the Ashburton Estate's agent called in Marryat saying that he was 'a man from Salisbury with over twenty years' experience of the Wylye and Till and a man no fisherman would argue with'. Marryat sided with the club which brought the problem to an end satisfactory to the members of the Wilton Club.

An interesting aside is that one of the members of the Kennet quadrilateral, Basil Field, designed an 'aerating bait-can' for which he was awarded a diploma at the Fisheries Exhibition. Cholmondeley-Pennell was so impressed by the can that he described it as an 'admirable invention'. It was made in two sizes by a Henry Bawcombe of Holloway, North London. It had thumb-operated bellows which provided the aeration as the angler walked along with the can in his hand, operating the bellows with his thumb to keep the live-bait in good order. Field was not the only innovative member of the quadrilateral.

Nathaniel Lloyd developed what he called a 'treble-grip rod ferrule', which he described in an article published in *The Field* of 25th September, 1897. He had produced a ferrule that would 'prevent the joints twisting round or coming apart. Americans maintain that plain ferrules (without dowels), if perfectly fitted, will not come apart, but it is doubtful whether 'suction' fittings would stand the severe test of dry-fly work. It is also questionable whether the 'perfect fit' would not vanish under such severe wear.' He produced 'metal fittings, which could be locked and unlocked at will, and should at the same time absolutely prevent the joints coming apart'. According to Halford : ' Messrs Hardy Brothers, of Alnwick, are the patentees and manufacturers of this ferrule, and I can add that having used it and seen it in use by Mr Lloyd and other friends for the last five years, I think it is the best fitting in the market.'

One of Marryat's good friends was Samuel Montagu (1832-1911), who became the first Baron Swaythling, was a successful merchant banker, philanthropist and one-time Liberal MP for the Whitechapel division of Tower Hamlets. He was born Montagu Samuel in Liverpool and was raised to a peerage in 1907. He was a one-time member of the Houghton Fly Fishing Club and a keen salmon fisherman and owned the Woodmill estate at South Stoneham and a stretch of the lower Itchen that included the famous Salmon Pool.

Another member of Halford's quadrilateral was William Quiller Orchardson, born Edinburgh, March 1832, who was a very important and successful painter; at the age of only sixteen he began to exhibit at the Royal Scottish Academy. He was very kind and sociable and very popular with everyone who knew him, characteristics which would have endeared him to the other members of the quadrilateral and Marryat. As a young man he had been very keen on sports, although he did give up hunting when he married in 1873, but remained a very keen angler and tennis player and was a very good billiards player too. He and his wife Ellen produced four sons and two daughters. He moved to London in 1862 and from the following year he exhibited annually at the Royal Academy. He was elected an associate of the Royal Academy in 1867 and ten years later he was elected a Royal Academician. Orchardson's painting based on an eyewitness account of Napoleon on Board the *Bellerophon*, the ship which carried him to exile on St Helena, caused a sensation when it was first exhibited in 1880. In 1897 he was appointed master of the Society of Portrait Painters and he painted Samuel Montagu's portrait. He was knighted in 1907 and died at his home in Portland Place, London, in April 1910.

The upper two miles of the Kennet fishery was characterised by 'a very great number of spawning shallows' and below this was what the quadrilateral referred to as the reserved water. Here there was a carrier running roughly parallel to the main river for about a mile and the fishing was limited to one bank only on the carrier with 'a concurrent right of fishing for guests of the freeholder'. The main river ran through the park surrounding the owner's house and fishing there was excluded from the lease. The two miles of the lower water consisted of a series of mill ponds which were 'sluggish, deep, and somewhat muddy, alternating with pretty shallows'. There were also many carriers and tributaries which extended the fishery quite considerably. Apart from the stretch of the by-stream, all other fishing was double bank.

The old Mill House was included in the twenty-one year lease and members of the quadrilateral and their families and fishing guests stayed there during the fishing season. They employed a housekeeper as well as two river keepers. The under-keeper's wage was increased from 17 shillings to 18 shillings a week in 1894.

Marryat managed to fish only once at Ramsbury, in 1895, on 14th June, in spite of receiving many invitations. And that day in June was to be the last time that he was to fish there. One event that was to prevent his fishing was a visit, towards the end of June, from his 'S American brother & his wife'. Herbert Charles had married Emma Grace, daughter of Edward Caird of Finnart, Garelochhead, on 6th April 1892.

Although he was not a member of the quadrilateral, Marryat volunteered to help Orchardson and Lloyd and the keepers and labourers with the spring pike netting in 1893. It was fortunate that Marryat was available as Halford had been stricken down with flu. Two hundred and ninety-five pike were netted in the middle and lower lengths. Most of them were jacks and very few fish were netted in the top stretch. In September, when the members were happy to stop fishing, they clear-cut all the weed and set to work to net the river thoroughly. Over two thousand pike were killed in 1893. The biggest weighed 10lb and only twenty weighed four pounds or more.

Halford was to write when the quadrilateral agreed to abandon their efforts to create a top flight fishery: 'When we gave it up the pike had been practically exterminated, and every yard of the river was fully stocked with trout of strains far superior to the indigenous slimy, yellow *Salmo fario* of the Kennet.'

The Rev. Patrick Murray Smythe, who was born in 1860, wrote extensive diaries on all his time spent fishing between 1872 and 1935. His last entry was just a fortnight before his death. Although he was twenty years younger, he met Marryat on 9th June, 1885, at the Deanery, Salisbury. He wrote: 'Arrived at the Deanery I found two very notable personages at tea - Doctor Boyd, better known as A.K.H.B., author of *The Recreations of a Country Parson*, and Mr Marryat, the best dry-fly fisherman in England.' He fished after dinner that evening when he caught 'a lanky old grayling of about 1lb' which he returned and a trout of 1¹/₂ lb 'from under the opposite bank'.

The next day Smythe joined Marryat and his old friend Tom Sanctuary 'in the punt and we pottered for some time together: though we did no good it was a real treat to see Marryat cast a dry fly and to handle his rod. He can cast eighty-seven feet with it.' In 1897 he had noted that the Frome at Stafford was 'a per-fect trout stream. Moreover the Frome is chock-full of trout and those considerable ones.'

Two years after first meeting Marryat, on 8th June, 1887, Patrick Smythe wrote in his diary:

On a lovely June morning I took the early train at Brockenhurst and arrived in due course at Horsebridge soon after ten to enjoy a day on the Houghton Club water. Houghton Club water is classic ground among dry-fly fishers where Halford, Mann [T. J. Mann, the brewer] and Marryat do disport themselves and where poor old Francis Francis cast his last earthly fly.

A friendly water-cress man guided me to the Mill at the bottom of the Houghton water and I put up my rod and nipped into my waders as soon as ever I could. An angler was smoking comfort-ably on the bridge, with whom I soon foregathered and found him to be no less a person than Mr Halford himself: and a very good friend I found him. He put me at once on to two trout who were rising at the head of the Mill pond and gave me a fly of his own dressing - (I think it was a Blue Up-right) - wherewith I rose both fish, but both were only slightly pricked. They seemed about 3lb. each. It was not long though before I was consoled, for in a bend just above I got a beautiful grayling of 2lb 10oz, the biggest ever I caught. Above this bend comes the 'Sheep's Bridge Shallow' - notissima fama - and above that curves, pools and shallows and a lovely island with a hut on it. So far I penetrated with Mr Halford in search of Mr Marryat who had gone upstream from here. Not finding him, we lunched. I spent most of the day round the Sheep's Bridge but beyond rising a dace or two and catching one little grayling and once again getting a meaningless splurge from a trout, I did nothing. Towards evening I foregathered with the Keeper and we went down together to a bit of water called 'Black Lake'. Here were fishing Marryat and Halford, each with a trout of near 3lb. They put me on to a rising fish, but I made two bad casts to begin, one short and one beyond, which caused Marryat to think very small potatoes of me - and say so! Most kindly they gave me one of their trout to keep my grayling company: and so we parted, they to dinner and the sedge-fly and I to the evening train.

6

In Pursuit of Grayling

One of the few documented times that Marryat fished elsewhere than the southern chalkstreams was in Derbyshire with
Francis Francis. (Hall suggested that Marryat also fished the
Eden and others report that he fished the Otter in Devon, perhaps whilst staying with Sanctuary when he was living in
Cornwall.) In his book *Angling Reminiscences*, Francis wrote
about fishing for trout and grayling in Derbyshire and although
he did not included any specific references to 'M', they did fish
there together. Francis and Marryat enjoyed winter grayling
fishing on the Test and Itchen in the days before many anglers
considered grayling to be vermin and that they should be exterminated. In the late 1880s and early in the next decade, the
Test held some memorable fish. One who discovered this fact
to his great delight, as well as the genuine pleasure of meeting
Marryat, was Francis M. 'Max' Walbran.

Max Walbran fished the river Test on 5th November, 1891,
a day that was to be what he described as one of the most
remarkable day's grayling fishing that he would ever experience.
He had been invited by his friend 'H' (F. M. Halford), a

member of the Houghton Club, to fish at Stockbridge for a few days. Walbran and 'H' left Waterloo Station on the afternoon of 4th November. 'Red Spinner' (William Senior) was to have joined them but was unable to at the last moment as bad cold had '[laid] him up by the heels'. But he did come to the station to see them off in spite of having described the expansion of the railway as having 'accomplished many wonders and over-come many difficulties. Steadily and surely it has intruded into the realms of romance and reduced them to its own utilitarian level'. The two-hour journey passed quickly with the two men no doubt deeply engrossed in talking about all matters to do with fly fishing and the sport to be had over the next few days. Walbran had heard and read so much about the big trout and grayling that were to be caught in the Test that he had accepted Halford's invitation with alacrity.

Walbran was born in 1852 and had his own fishing tackle and sporting goods shop in Leeds. He was a very regular con-tributor to *The Field* (possibly as a result of his friendship with Red Spinner), the *Fishing Gazette* and *The Angler* as well as local newspapers. He also wrote books, including *The British Angler* and *Grayling and How to Catch Them*. He was swept to his death wading when fishing a North Country spate river for grayling on 15th February, 1909.

As well as being seen off at Waterloo, the two were met at Stockbridge by Major Carlisle. The three were to stay at The Vine - 'a real comfortable old-fashioned hostelry' - and once installed, they were soon enjoying a good meal. The evening was spent reminiscing about earlier fishing exploits, Carlisle's experiences of the Indian Mutiny and plans for the next day's sport. Carlisle observed that the grayling had not been seen rising to the fly of late and he suggested that Walbran should try a worm in the bottom Hatch Hole where he was confident that he would land a good fish or two. Arrangements for the next day were agreed - Walbran and 'H' were to drive the two and a half miles to the Mill and 'our friend' was to come by train to Horsebridge where the three would meet. They finished their whiskies and smoked their last cigars of the evening before retiring for the night.

Walbran was awake bright and early, long before it was light. It was what he considered to be a good grayling day: sharp and frosty. After breakfast, they were off to the river by 9 o'clock. As they crossed the bridge over the Test at the end of Stockbridge's long, wide street, Walbran had his first view of the river and stood up in the trap to admire the shallows below the bridge and the crystal clear water. They soon passed the Machine Barn on the left, "Beyond that meadow is the shallow named after it, which Francis Francis used to mention so often in his articles," said 'H'. This and a second visit that Walbran 'paid to that district' were to remain what he described as 'a green spot' in his memory; he said he would 'always remember the Hatch Hole at Houghton Mill, "Boot Island" and that memorable November day'.

During the race week and the coursing meeting later in the season, Stockbridge was 'full to overflowing with aristocratic visitors'. But that November day there were no crowds to impede their progress to the mill. The drive was two and a half miles along a country lane where the wonderful autumn colours of the leaves had not disappeared. The hedgerows were brightened with scarlet berries and hips and haws. They passed the Boot Inn in Houghton and as they went round a corner they saw Houghton Mill for the first time. Dismounting from their trap, they stood on the bridge, looking into the mill pool but they could not see any sign of a fish nor a rise.

As Walbran was getting his tackle ready, Halford came over and remarked quietly, "I should advise you, master, to use something stouter than this," while examining Walbran's fine drawn gut cast, "for if you hook a good fish he will break you to a certainty." But Walbran was confident in his choice as he had already landed two-pound grayling with the same tackle on the Costa.

Halford's advice to Walbran to use thicker gut brings to mind his enthusiasm for telling many of his fellow anglers what tackle or fly to use. On one occasion, in early September, 1891, Skues and 'an angling friend from the British Museum' agreed to fish the Abbotts Barton stretch of the Itchen. Skues was recovering from a debilitating illness that had left him feeling pretty low and uncertain as to how long he might live but fortunately ten days on the Yore had seen him restored to better health. In his story 'Shocks and a Lesson' (published in *Itchen Memories*), Skues recounted how 'We had heard on the day of our arrival in Winchester that the great man [Halford] was putting up at the George and was nightly welcoming his worshippers at that hotel to hear him expound the pure and authentic gospel of the dry fly which no one would dream of questioning.' Skues had been given a copy, in 1887, of Halford's *Floating Flies and How to Dress Them* and a first edition, in 1889, of Halford's *Dry-Fly Fishing in Theory and Practice*, and as both Skues and his friend were 'relatively inexperienced, [they] looked on these immortal works as revelation from on high with all the authority of gospel truth'. During the course of the evening 'It came to our ears . . . that we were to have the great man's company on the Abbotts Barton water, the lessee having invited him for a week'.

The next day Skues and his friend arrived at the river a short time before their 'mentor'. Skues' friend decided to fish above the Duck's Nest Spinney and Skues went downstream, leaving the main river 'to the great man'. Halford soon came into view and Skues was able to see him casting on Winnel Water. He then crossed the meadow between the main river and the feeder stream and 'accosted' Skues 'from the left bank of the side stream to advise us kindly on the fly to put up, and to make his advice clearer he cast his fly to light on the right bank of the side stream, having first ascertained that I had mounted a fly of George Holland's dressing, known as the Quill Marryat.' Some years later Skues referred to his fly as a Little Marryat. He had made his choice of fly 'based on little pale duns seen on the water'. Halford insisted that his choice of fly 'which was an India-rubber olive' was correct. Anyway, Skues 'took a look at his fly and was not a little shocked to see how coarse was the gut on which his fly was tied, but I was also too polite or timid to venture on such a comment'.

The three of them met at lunch-time when Halford asked Skues how he had got on that morning. Skues had caught two and a half brace while the great expert had but one trout only. 'Halford only fished the Abbotts Barton length for three more days of this week, but just as I had been profoundly shocked to do better than the great master did on the first day, I was fated to be similarly shocked on each of his three other days.' The lesson that Skues learnt on those days was that it is better to rely on one's own powers of observation and 'not to attach undue importance to authority'. Incidentally, his friend who caught only one fish had the pleasure of it being the biggest of the week at 1lb 13oz.

The one person Halford would have been well advised not to treat in such a patrician manner was Marryat who would surely have thanked him so kindly for his (un)welcome advice with a pithy piece of advice of his own. There are times and ways and means of giving a fellow angler help - particularly when it is obvious that they are making a mess of things - but Halford seems to have lacked any such sensitivity. His advice was well meant but not always delivered in a manner to endear the recipient to him.

Back at Houghton Mill on that frosty November day, a boy

in the mill yard was asked to get the anglers some 'gilt tails' and he soon returned with a good quantity in 'an old lobster tin'. 'H' then went and asked the miller to close one of the two hatches through which the river was flowing into the mill pool and to adjust the other so that 'the stream was running through the pool to our liking'. Walbran then set his 'wee red topped float' to what he estimated to be the required depth and took his 'first swim on a Hampshire chalkstream'. When he made his third cast, the float dipped and he felt something heavy on the end of his line. 'Twenty yards of line was taken in the first rush, and then down the fish went to the bottom and stuck there. Ten minutes of grand sport ensued, when H. cleverly netted him - a grand trout between two and three pounds.' He was unhooked and returned to the river above the hatch so as not to upset other fish in the pool. The next half hour saw no further action so they crossed the hatch and stood on the opposite bank. 'Then the fun began.' His first swim produced a grayling of 1lb 11 oz and 'within an hour four even larger ones were laid beside him on the grass'.

H. left two visible and hid the rest just as 'South West' [Major Carlisle] appeared in sight.

"Ah!" He [South West] exclaimed, on observing the brace of fish, "I am glad you have done something; you may consider yourself fortunate to have done so well in so short a time."

"And how about these, old man?" said H., uncovering the other three.

Walbran went on to catch twelve grayling from the mill pool, weighing a total of 22lb 1oz, with the biggest fish weighing in at 2lb 6oz and the smallest 1lb 8oz. Neither Halford nor 'South West' fished and were happy to look after Walbran who also caught eight trout of between two and three pounds. He was broken by three fish but he wrote that 'With such extremely fine tackle it was utterly impossible to expect to land every fish without disaster'. As darkness fell the trap arrived to take the happy anglers back to the 'cosy inn'.

The next morning two telegrams were delivered to them, one of which was from Red Spinner saying that he could not join them. The other was 'from M. - prince of dry fly fishers - to intimate that he was coming [from Salisbury] to spend the day in our company'. Max Walbran was twelve years younger than Marryat and it would have been a rare privilege to fish with a truly great man who was at the height of his fishing powers and expertise. Although he had done so well with worms the day before, Walbran wanted to try fishing with a fly and so they gave the Hatch Hole a rest and walked upstream. Some good fish, including both trout and grayling, were showing by the Sheep Bridge. Walbran was to write:

M. soon joined us, and then, for the first time, I saw an angler who could do anything he liked with rod and line. I have met many men in my time, but I can truthfully say never one with half the sweet disposition, or true sportsmanlike feelings, possessed by him. To know him is a pleasure, and if for nothing else, I am thankful that providence made me a born angler, so that I have within the past thirty years made the acquaintance of him and others whom to know is a privilege. It was only by the intercession of H. that I was allowed to witness his marvellous 'steeple cast', by which he can keep twenty yards of line towering like a corkscrew in the air, and then shoot a midge-fly across the stream, when it floats like a thing of life. Then he performed the same feat left-handed; then threw the fly behind his back; and then under his leg, in each case the fly floating perfectly. This was worth going from Yorkshire to Hampshire to see, without anything else. Of our fishing on the second day, the less said the better. M. would not

*fish, I couldn't, and H. landed two goodly grayling, 1lb 12oz and
2lb 3oz respectively.*

It is worth bearing in mind that Marryat's casting demonstration was performed at a time when anglers still 'whipped' rivers
and streams, rather than casting a fly in a manner that would
be understood today. *The Field* announced that the new angling
editor, Francis Francis, was 'a fisherman who had "whipped half
the streams of the United Kingdom" '. Marryat's ability with a
fly rod suggests that he had a real understanding of the mechan-
ics of fly casting and that casting and presenting a fly delicately
was not simply a process of whipping rod and line backwards
and forwards at high speed.

The next day, the 7th, was to be a red letter day for Max
Walbran. He was to catch two grayling that together tipped the
scales at a remarkable 6lb 9oz. When they arrived at the mill
pool at Houghton Mill, Halford encouraged Walbran to have
one more try with a worm before going upstream and trying the
fly. Walbran started fishing from the same spot where, on the
5th, he had had 'such grand sport'. He soon hooked something
heavy on his third swim through the pool.

*H., standing on the weir beam, saw the fish turn over, and when
I expressed my opinion that he was something larger than anything
I had yet seen he nonchalantly remarked, "About 2lb, I think." I
thought differently, for I could literally do nothing with him. For
fully ten minutes he kept the float quite out of sight, and then a roll
over on top revealed his splendid proportions.*

"Now, then," I exclaimed triumphantly, "Did you see that?"

*"No use attempting to deceive you any longer," said my com-
panion. "I saw when you hooked him what he was, but did not
wish to unnerve you. He is the biggest grayling I have ever seen;
now do take care."*

Walbran was still struggling to get to terms with the fish after twenty minutes. He remembered Halford's comment on the fineness of his gut and was starting to worry that his cast would be chafed and give way. As he felt that it was unlikely he would be able to play it out and net it himself, a different approach to landing the fish was required. Halford went and lay down on the wall by the weir and proceeded to sink his landing-net, deep into the water. The plan was that Walbran would endeavour to lead the grayling over the net which Halford would lift, with the fish in it. Any fisherman reading this will see immediately the major flaws in this strategy! However, Walbran was eventually able to coax the fish in the required direction and draw him over the net. Just as the fish was about to set off on another boring run, Halford raised the net and was able to deposit the startled and surprised fish on the bank.

What I did I cannot say. I believe I nearly embraced H., and then came the question - 'What does he weigh?' The balance proclaimed 3lb 9oz - the largest grayling ever landed on that water . . . After the episode described above we sat on the weir beam smoking for fully half an hour.

Once they had recovered, they made their way upstream to Boot Island just above which was a 'beautiful gravely shallow' where they could see three or four large fish 'leisurely sucking down every insect that the eddy above floated down to them'. Halford was very keen for Walbran to have a go for one of them but he laughed at the idea. However, he managed to persuade Halford to tie on a gold-ribbed hare's ear which he proceeded to float over the group of grayling. Walbran wrote:

The result was tantalising. The fish were not put down, but continued taking the naturals just as before - the artificial they

*would have none of. After, perhaps, twenty casts, H. got a little bit
disgusted, but I prevailed on him to have just one more throw. Up
came the biggest fish of the lot, as though the fly was quite a novelty. The next moment H. was rushing downstream like an express
train, and I after him with a net. Over two hedges and a stile we
tumbled and then, just as the fish was going under a foot bridge, I
netted him, a handsome grayling of 3lb weight.*

That was the fish that provided the three pounds for the total
weight of 6lb 9oz.

This was to be Max Walbran's last opportunity to fish this
particular part of the Test as the Houghton Club came to an
end and the waters it fished were bought by the new Stockbridge Club.

Francis and Marryat went grayling fishing one December day
when they fished what would seem - based on Halford's
description - to have been the Sheepbridge shallows on the Test.
Marryat was rigging his rod, standing on the bridge, when he
spotted a large grayling. "There's a three-pound grayling gone
up - a real big one!" he said. Although there were often grayling
of at least two pounds on the shallows, a 3-pounder was
uncommon. Francis saw the fish himself, but not clearly, and
'once or twice saw the wave of a big fish across the shallow, and,
regardless of grammar I cried, "That's him!" ' When Francis
started fishing he hooked a big grayling that took him on a
merry dance downstream, forcing him to cross a number of
'drawns'. To cross one, Marryat found a hard gravelly spot that
was about twenty-five yards away from the river. Francis was
thankful that he was fishing with a long double-handed rod as
'A shorter rod would have been fatal here' as it would have been
very difficult to keep his line clear of the field and bank. Once
back by the side of the river he got sight of the fish. "By Jove,
he's the big one," he whispered to himself. Fortunately for Fran-

cis he now had about forty yards of clear bank to battle with the fish. But as soon as Francis started to draw him into the bank 'he laid his head out, flapped his tail, waggled that great dorsal fin, and out he went again to mid-stream, and down, down he dropped, till I had to negotiate a third draw, complicated by a beastly set of rails on the further side.' After more dramas Francis was eventually able to draw the fish over his net and lift him clear of the water, something like a hundred yards downstream from where he had hooked him. When he and Marryat weighed the fish, the scales reached just 3lb. Fortunately for Francis he had hooked the fish 'in the extreme upper lip, which is a trifle less breakable than the palate' with what he described as a midge fly which he had been fishing wet.

7

Not the Fly but the Driver

Marryat was very happy to be the life and soul of the party when amongst his friends. He would talk and tell yarns into the night long after the time 'when the bedroom candlestick should have been lit'. 'Marryat was full of wit and repartee, and his conversation abounded in *bons mots*, but he would have been the last to wish this little joke to be taken *au grand sérieux*' was how Halford described 'one of the best friends I ever had'. But he was not prepared to be a public entertainer merely to satisfy someone else's whim.

Marryat's doctor friend, Tom Sanctuary, knew him as a many-sided man who 'as a reader and raconteur was not often excelled in private life'. Although he was never persuaded to write anything for publication on fly fishing, he wrote 'some good sonnets', was very well-read and 'knew his Shakespeare pretty well by heart'. When amongst friends he was the life and soul of the party and 'enjoying as he did an unlimited command of facial expression and original phraseology, it may be easily imaged what an acquisition he was to any social gathering'. However, he was apparently 'reserved by nature, essentially the student, and disliked above all things to be "drawn" or trotted out for any but his most intimate friends'. This would explain his refusal to 'perform' on one of the very rare occasions that he did attend a dinner at the Flyfishers' Club, in London.

Red Spinner wrote how all attempts to get him to address members at the annual dinner of the Flyfishers' Club (which he always refused to join) failed. But Senior really put his foot in it in 1889 when making a speech at the annual dinner:

You have often read in the angling magazines and newspapers references to a great master in the art of dry-fly fishing, who is always called 'M'. (Hear, hear!) He, I am happy and proud to say, is in our company tonight, and all who know him will agree with what all the keepers in the West of England and all practical men will tell you, that he is the finest dry-fly fishermen in the world. (Applause.)

Sadly for the members of the Club, Marryat was not persuaded to respond and never attended another dinner. Four years earlier, in 1885, R. B. Marston had written to him on 5th January to ask him if he 'would help us with the Flyfishers' Club', just then established. Marryat replied in his humorous way that he could not join, but that he would be happy to contribute 'a big wooden spade as a prize for the biggest fish story-teller'. According to Marston he did take a considerable interest in the club over the years, but from afar.

'South West' noted that Marryat was the life and soul of shooting house parties - at the dining table, in the smoking room and also in the billiards room, where, in the words of Sanctuary 'he played a capital game of billiards'. Marryat was apparently a good and very safe shot and the two shot together regularly.

A little time after Marryat and Halford met for the first time, when they were staying at the 'dear old mill at Houghton' and Marryat, who 'was as full of spirits and harmless jokes as a boy, seized the opportunity of Francis's being late for breakfast to place empty egg shells, with the unbroken ends turned upwards, before Francis's plate. Loud was the explosion of laughter when the latter discovered the little trick that had been played upon him. He knew at once who was the author, and with a "What a confounded child you are, Marryat," joined in the merriment'.

The famous story about the fly and the driver happened when Marryat, Francis Francis, Halford and William Turle (who had a slightly different version of the story) and others were fishing the Old Barge at Winchester (possibly in 1882), 'a dozen rods or so in a very limited amount of space'. Marryat was on the extreme right and Francis at the other end of the line of anglers. Marryat was catching fish with great regularity while poor old Francis could not get even an offer. In an endeavour to improve his sport, Francis asked for a message to be passed down the line to Marryat: "What fly are you killing with?" After the question had been repeated to him, as quick as a flash Marryat replied: "The driver." This was passed back along the line to Francis. Francis was reluctant to admit that he had never heard of a pattern called the driver and asked the next man down to thank Marryat for the information. Francis then proceeded to change his fly as though the information that he had been given was of use. He still did not get a rise and did not kill a trout all day while Marryat had a basket of two or three brace.

Halford's account of the incident was that it came to a head after dinner that evening. Francis asked Marryat: "What on earth did that silly message about the fly mean?" Marryat replied:

"I was told that Francis wanted the name of the fly I was killing with, and I replied 'the driver'."

"*Yes,*" *remarked Francis,* "*that was the message I received; but what fly is it? I do not know such a pattern.*"

"*You silly old chump!*" *said Marryat,* "*can't you see? Not the fly, but the driver.*"

Today most fly fishermen know full well the importance of presentation. It is also worth pointing out that a fly was a form of horse-drawn transport let out for hire, such as a hansom cab or similar two-wheel carriage drawn by a single horse, so Marryat's remark was a play on words as well. Visitors to his uncle's farm at Langham, Norfolk, had to take 'a rumbling fly' from the nearby town of Holt to the village. Lord Grey used to take a half-hour drive in a one-horse fly from Winchester station to the nearest point that was accessible by wheels to the cottage that he built on the Itchen in 1890.

Major Turle recounted a story that has a surprisingly familiar ring to it at a time when so-called yuppies and city slickers were taking up fly fishing because it was the 'thing to do'. The story concerned Marryat's own description of how he fished, delivered on the riverbank to a 'London novice'.

The young man in question, got up in the latest and most approved of fishing costumes, with rod, net, and basket all new, was not having a lively time on Hammond's weekly ticket, and asked Marryat how it was he was so successful. The latter, who saw the fellow was an utter ignoramus, on whom it was not worth while wasting invaluable information, replied with the solemn, earnest expression he knew so well how to assume at will: "First I chuck at them with my right hand, and then with my left; if that won't do, I fish them under my leg; and, as a last chance, I have a go at them behind my back. But if that fails, I just leave them to their own devices, and start off in search of another rising fish." In blank dismay the would-be fisherman returned to the Royal, packed up his things, and, regardless of the loss of his week's ticket, set off for town that same evening, where no doubt he entertained his friends with accounts of the strange manner of fishing practised on the Itchen.

* * *

In his reminiscences of Marryat, published in the *Fishing Gazette* of 29th February, 1896, but published first in *The Field*, following the great man's death, Red Spinner wrote: 'It must have been close upon thirty years ago that I first heard about Marryat's prowess in casting a fly.' When Senior had been fishing Winnal Water, 'in old John Hammond's time', he mentioned the name of a fellow angler who he considered to be 'one of the best casters of a trout fly' that he knew. Hammond's response was immediate: "Oh!" he said, "you had better wait till you see Mr Marryat; he can hook a fly into any straw you like in that hayrick." Red Spinner wrote: 'As the hayrick was about seventy yards distant I knew this to be speaking in parables, but not a long time afterwards I saw for myself what a superb hand with the trout rod Marryat was.' A friend of Major Turle claimed that Marryat 'was the only man I ever met who could throw a fly across the Old Barge in an east wind'. What was described as a peculiarity at the time, was his penchant for holding his rod with his forefinger extended along the top of the handle, pointing towards the rod tip.

Sanctuary described Marryat as 'far and away the most accurate "caster" as I have ever seen'. According to Sanctuary Marryat could place 'a fly between twigs and leaves with the utmost facility, and this with either hand indifferently'. He accredited his 'extreme accuracy' to casting with his forefinger along the top of the rod handle. Marryat told Sanctuary that when he first started casting with that grip that it placed considerable strain on his fingers but as he got used to it, the strength in his fingers increased. Halford described the way that he held his fly rod: 'Marryat gripped his rod with both thumb and forefinger pressed against the handle and pointed upwards. He had an abnormally long forefinger; possibly this was to some extent the effect of this peculiar grip. He always considered that this grip gave him greater power of directing the line and fly with extreme accuracy.' Major Turle also commented on Marryat's grip, with the 'forefinger straight up the butt' but did not mention his thumb. Turle found the grip to be very uncomfortable, painful in fact, but he imagined that once a caster had mastered it, it would give added power to a cast.

Sanctuary claimed to have seen Marryat drop 'a fly on a sixpence three times out of four with twenty yards of line, provided there was no wind. This I have seen him do on more than one occasion at Salisbury'. But his fly fishing was not completely fault free. Sanctuary maintained that Marryat was 'a bit too rough on his fish, both in striking and playing them' and seemed to feel that deluding a fish into taking his fly was the main objective and landing it very secondary. In his letter on quill bodies for flies, published in *The Field* of 8th January, 1881, Marryat wrote that he disagreed with Ronald that 'a fish spits out a hard-bodied fly of quill or hair quicker than a soft-bodied one of fur or dubbing', and then continued, 'Anyway, if he does, it is good enough for me if I can get him to take it into his mouth at all'. He rarely, if ever, hammered a fish - that is, cast repeatedly to the same fish - if it refused his offer after two or three casts.

Halford, when describing how to perform the steeple cast in *Dry-Fly Fishing, Theory and Practice*, noted: 'The distance to be accomplished after a little practice, by means of this style of throwing, is quite astonishing to the fisherman himself.' Marryat was capable of casting more than thirty yards on a calm day. Halford also repeated one of Marryat's comments on casting:

'A silent rod and a whistling line mean good casting', but he added that when throwing against the wind a soft 'whoosh' of the rod is often heard. It may be laid down as an axiom that nine anglers out of ten put too much energy into their casting, and forget to allow the rod to do its fair share of the work.

Halford also quoted a different version of the same saying, which he heard from Nathaniel Lloyd:

Mr Lloyd remarks on this : 'The late Mr Marryat used to say that the rod should be silent and the line sing. I find, however, that the rod always makes a noise if held so that the rings are in front. If, on the other hand, the rod is turned so that the rings lie above or underneath there is no sound from the rod, the line only being heard. Mr Marryat often fished thus, which would account for his mistaken idea.'

During the time that Marryat and Halford were fishing together, the argument was still raging as to whether or not a single-handed rod was the better tool for casting to trout or the increasingly 'old-fashioned' two handed or double-handed rod. Halford was of the opinion that the 'small single-handed rod' was the best tool for the job although his old friend Francis Francis, whose 'opinions have carried and ever must carry very great weight with all fly fishermen' had always been an advocate of the double-hander. This was a constant topic of conversation for the three of them both during and at the end of a day's fishing. While they could never agree, Marryat and Halford did concede that the longer double-hand rod might make longer casts 'through being able to hold up a much longer line, and not being as liable to catch the long grass behind the angler' and that such a rod would give 'more command over a hooked fish'. Marryat was heard to observe dryly that 'You can't make a fly talk with a double-handed rod'. In a footnote to the section of the chapter on casting in *A Book on Angling*, Francis wrote: 'I have seen twenty-six yards cast with a single-handed rod, and I also cast that length at the same time and with the same line and rod. It was on the Old Barge river at Winchester that that was done, my friend Mr Marryat being the other operator, and it was with his rod and line. I have heard of even longer casts than this.'

Marryat could cast with either hand and was always happy to demonstrate his casting skills and perform tricks such as casting sideways under his outstretched leg. He also did all the casting for the photographs (taken by Elliott and Fry and subsequently turned into drawings by Moul) in Halford's book *Dry-Fly Fishing, Theory and Practice*, quite often with his left hand in his jacket pocket and not using it to control the line. Halford drew his readers' 'careful attention' to the plates 'because they are not in any way fancied or fanciful illustrations of what any one wishing to prove his own particular theory may think he has seen, but are actual reproductions of instantaneous photographs taken for the purpose of illustrating this work'. (In his later books, a very stiff and wooden-looking Halford can be seen demonstrating the various casts.) William Senior wrote that even though these drawings showed only Marryat's back view; he had 'such a striking personality that even the back views are portraits of the man to all who knew him'. The tam o'shanter was a bit of a giveaway as to the identity of the caster.

These images of Marryat caught the eyes of two girls anxious to learn to fish who Senior wrote about in his book *Lines in Pleasant Places* in a chapter entitled 'Angling Cousins at The Vicarage'. The girls had a cousin who brought some fishing books for them to study but it was the illustrations in 'Mr Halford's Marryat edition of *Dry Fly Fishing* that pinned their attention to that work for at least two hours. They wondered

not a little at the attitude of the dry-fly gentleman as he is photographed doing the overhand cast, downward cut, steeple cast,
and dry-switch.' Senior also noted that 'one of the two readers'
was 'a kodakeer [photographer] of no mean skill'.

When fishing, Marryat would always accept the challenge of
a rising fish in an apparently impossible position, often one
where no other angler would dream of trying a cast. And probably to the annoyance of some of his fishing companions, he
usually seems to have been successful in most of these cases. A
lesser man would, no doubt, have earned himself a reputation
as a show-off but this did not happen with Marryat. He obviously had a very generous spirit and, I am sure, set about
catching difficult fish as an encouragement to others and to
show that there were few fish that really could not be attacked
successfully with a fly rod. A good example of this was given
by Arthur N. Gilbey in his contribution, 'A Talk About It', to
the book *The Book of The Fly Rod* which was edited by H. T.
Sheringham and John C. Moore. Gilbey was a member of the
gin-distilling family and a long-time member of the Houghton
Club and, by repute, a very hard fisherman who according to
J. W. Hills caught sixty-six trout weighing 136lb 4 oz during a
six-day period in 1906. Lunn's Particular was, indirectly, named
after him by its inventor, William Lunn, the famous Test river
keeper. Gilbey was fishing Park Stream one day and having a
difficult time. He told Lunn that 'The trout are too particular
today'. Lunn then produced one of his new flies and suggested
that Gilbey should try it. Gilbey proceeded to catch three fish
with it before the short rise was over. Gilbey asked Lunn what
the fly was called and was told that it was Lunn's Particular.
This incident took place in 1917 when the word 'particular'
was a popular term for a man's favourite tipple. Lunn, whose
father had once worked in a distillery, had thus made a clever
joke in telling a gin distiller that the fly was his particular.

Gilbey wrote that he remembered Marryat well and that he was certainly one of the greatest anglers he had ever known and a great man.

He would catch fish when nobody else could, and his casting was wonderful. He used to come down with a great bundle of rods - dozens of them - and great heavy gun-metal reels. But he taught me a lot. I remember when I was fishing with him one day, and there was a fish rising round the corner of a bush. I knew I couldn't reach it, so I asked Marryat to show me how to do it. Flick-flick and he'd risen it and hooked it; a most miraculous cast. Then he asked me to play it, saying it was really my fish; but I said no, he'd caught it and he must play it - whereupon he planted the spear of his rod in the ground and left it. So I picked up his rod and played his fish, and in the end I landed it.

(Many years ago fly rods were supplied with a metal spear that could be fixed to the butt-end of the rod by removing the rubber button at the bottom end of the handle. The rodmaker Hardy designed a reversible spear and button that allowed the spear to be stored inside the rod handle. With the spear in position, a rod could be left standing vertical.)

But Marryat did have his failures. Francis Francis recounted one such incident in a story in *The Field* to illustrate the fact that a previously-hooked fish would continue to rise to the natural fly. Marryat was casting to a feeding fish on the Test which he rose and lost, leaving his fly in its mouth. The fish continued to rise and Francis himself had a go at it and although it came for his fly, he failed to set the hook. Marryat then took his turn and also tempted the fish. This went on for quite some time until one of them got hung up on a post upstream from where the fish was rising. As Marryat did not want to leave half his cast blowing in the breeze, he went to disentangle it which had the effect of frightening the fish.

However, when other anglers were struggling he did his best to help and was able to identify why an angler was having trouble casting. One July day Marryat and Halford were fishing at Houghton when there was a goodly downstream wind blowing. Halford rounded a bend above Houghton lodge to be confronted by a fish rising steadily, taking every dun that passed within reach of it. Halford struggled to cast into the wind and spent two hours trying to catch the fish which was still rising. Obviously he never got his fly close enough to it to put it down. Eventually Marryat returned from upstream to see how his friend was getting on. By this time Halford was 'utterly disheartened . . . hot, tired, and of course casting with more force and more rapidly at each failure'. Marryat's assessment of what Halford was doing wrong came quickly: 'Steady, go slow and do not use so much force.' When Halford started to follow this advice, Marryat advised Halford to 'finish your chuck with the rod point on the water'. Halford then 'made a slow easy cast and dropped the point of the rod, and to my utter astonishment the fly landed just right. The fish came up and rose but I was so surprised at the success of the cast that I never raised my hand and did not even prick the fish.' Halford was able to thank Marryat for his help and advice, delivered with great patience. He thought that for the first time in his fishing life he had 'acquired the art, and now felt that I could cast against any reasonable wind that blew'. He attributed his success entirely to Marryat's advice and tuition.

In his review of the life of Halford, published in *Salmon and Trout Magazine*, number 54, January 1929, Skues opened his remarks by writing: 'The days when Frederic Maurice *(sic)* Halford bestrode the fly-fishing world like a giant with none to say him "nay" are no more. Time has brought its inevitable revenges and, with questioning of some of his doctrine, there

has obtruded of late a disposition to belittle the essential service which he did to fly-fishing.' Although he completed his
opening paragraph by saying that his intention was to set down
the 'true nature of his achievement', when Halford was alive
and Skues was developing the art of nymph fishing for chalkstream trout, the two had a difficult and somewhat testy
relationship. Skues had been a harsh critic of many of Halford's ideas although they did fish together and Halford had
offered to sponsor, along with William Senior, Skues' membership of the Flyfishers' Club. So if Skues was really intent
on examining and setting forth the true nature of Halford's
achievement, it seems strange that he then wrote: 'The fact
stands, that of all that group of angling supermen, Halford was
the one upon whom the genius of Marryat fastened for the
performance of the great work.' At first this seems to have been
a solitary view of Halford's life but when Red Spinner wrote in
The Field 'A glance at any of the books written by Mr Halford,
who is the present Gamaliel of the school, will show that in all
his experiments and achievements he sat at the feet of his
friend Marryat' it would seem to support and confirm Skues'
opinion of Marryat's career and place in the development of
dry-fly fishing in the nineteenth century. Another comment
that would seem to offer support to Skues's opinion was the
opening paragraph of an article, 'How I Won My Spurs', written by 'HMD' and published in the *Journal of the Fly-fishers'
Club*, Summer, 1932. HMD wrote: 'In the late Seventies of
the last century, what time Mr Frederic Halford was a junior
member of the old Houghton Club, sitting at the feet of that
great master, George Sewlyn Marryat.' In his article Skues
continued in a similar vein, describing 'the magnificent justification of Marryat's choice of Halford to be the prophet of
the new cult'. Earlier, in 1923, Skues had written that Marryat
'died leaving behind him probably the most uncontested

reputation ever enjoyed in the history of trout fishing for supremacy as a practitioner of that art and having, on the confession of F. M. Halford, exercised upon that writer the predominating influence which gave us the body of his work on the dry fly and its entomology . . . It is in the work of his friend, "Detached Badger", that G. S. Marryat's record is to be found.'

A few years earlier in *The Way of a Trout With a Fly* Skues had written that, in his opinion, it was the introduction of the 'heavy American braided oiled silk line and the split-cane rod' that made the dry fly possible as it was then a practical proposition to attempt to cast *into* the wind. 'With the hour came the men, Mr H. S.Hall, Mr G. S. Marryat, and Mr F. M. Halford, who evolved from the poor feeble types of dry fly of the [eighteen] seventies the efficient dry fly of the eighties and the present day.'

Another writer whose opinions on the place of Marryat in fly-fishing history, support Skues' contention, was Joseph Keen. He wrote of the 'great influence' that Marryat had on 'Halford, Francis Francis, Hall, Dunne, William Lunn, Roger Wolley - too many have had to be left out for it to be a proper history'. In the next paragraph in his book, *Fluorescent Flies*, he again refers to Halford having been 'influenced greatly' by Marryat.

In his contribution on fishing for brown trout in chalkstreams in *The Complete Fly-Fisher*, first published in 1963, Major Oliver Kite wrote on dry fly fishing:

In late Victorian times, a number of scholarly and inventive fly-fishers with enviable opportunities to fish the classic waters of the great chalkstreams like the Test, the Kennet and the Itchen, evolved a pattern of chalkstream fishing, the influence of which has persisted to this day. Francis Francis and G. S. Marryat set the stage for the more detailed work of F.M. Halford who, more than anyone else, formulated the cult of the dry fly, made feasible by H.S. Hall's invention of the eyed hook.

(Crediting the invention of the eyed hook to Hall is a surprising error for a man as knowledgeable as Kite.) How much of this statement was Kite's own opinion and how much was it influenced by the earlier comments of Skues? Kite was a student of the development of fly fishing, particularly upstream nymph fishing, and so was able to reach his own opinions but it is also strange that this seems to be the only time that he mentioned the name of Marryat, and that of Francis, in his writings.

8

'Aunt Harryat'

As a brother to six sisters and father of three daughters, Marryat was obviously well used to being with girls of a wide range of ages. During Halford's tenancy of the Kennet fishery, he spent time with Basil Field, a successful London solicitor, and his two daughters, Daisy, who was aged thirteen in 1893 at the start of Halford's tenancy, and Myrtle who was two years younger. Daisy was a remarkable young girl who announced after meeting Nathaniel Lloyd for the first time that he was the man she was going to marry. Not only did she know what she wanted throughout her life, she also got it. She was to marry Nathaniel Lloyd, the youngest member of the quadrilateral, in 1905. The guidebook to the house and estate of Great Dixter, where she lived with Nathaniel and which she continued to run after his death until her own in 1972, described her as 'his formidable widow'.

Nathaniel Lloyd had an interesting life. He was born on 5th March, 1867, in Manchester. Following his education, one of his first jobs was managing the advertising and printing for the Mazzawattee Tea Co. and then, in 1893, he founded Nathaniel

Lloyd & Company, Lithographic Printers, in Blackfriars, south London. He made a great success of the business, retired from the company in 1909 and then, with his brother, became joint managing director of the Star Bleaching Company, Manchester, until 1912. Business commitments meant that he could fish only at the weekends. He married Daisy in 1905 and they produced and raised six children.

In his later years Lloyd studied and then practised architecture and became a Fellow of the Royal Institute of British Architects in 1931, two years before his death. He was much influenced by Sir Edwin Lutyens RA, whom he employed to manage an extensive programme of restoration and enlargement of Great Dixter, the mediaeval house in Northiam, East Sussex, that he bought in 1910. Works involved moving a complete mediaeval hall house from Benenden in Kent and re-building it at Great Dixter. Lloyd went on to write books on architectural history, English country houses and garden design - he had a keen interest in topiary - and built a significant collection of photographs of the history and evolution of the English country house. He taught himself architectural photography and became a very accomplished architectural photographer taking photographs of a standard better than many of the professionals of his day. His photographic collection, much of which was stored under the billiard table at Great Dixter, demonstrated an extraordinary knowledge of architectural detail which gives it much of its significance and importance today. In *Who Was Who* his recreations were listed as fly fishing (Marryat taught him everything that he knew and he went on to be equally accomplished), shooting, golf, billiards and, rather interestingly, joinery.

Nathaniel and Daisy's last born, Christopher, inherited his mother's passion for gardens and gardening which she had had from an early age. He grew up to became a very well-respected and important gardening writer and gardened with great passion with his mother up to her death (in 1972), and continued to manage and develop the gardens at his family home until his own death in January 2006.

As Marryat had declined to join the Halford quadrilateral on the Kennet, he was only able to fish there as a guest, joining the house party at the Mill House in Ramsbury which was then a large but quiet village. Marryat arrived at Ramsbury on 8th June for the first time during the quadrilateral's first season and stayed for three days.

Daisy Field arrived at the Mill House, with her mother and sister, on 6th May and she was soon busying herself in the domestic arrangements and started to make a garden for herself. Even at such a young age, she was very observant of people and their ways and she recorded in her diary her father's early less than successful efforts at fly fishing: 'We go fishing with Papa but catch nothing but huge minnows. He comes home with his tail between his legs.' Daisy and her sister Myrtle had the honour of being taken fishing by Halford himself. When he hooked a fish, he handed the rod to Daisy to play it but she lost it very quickly. She then went on to land a fish which he caught later in the day. Daisy succeeded in catching her first fish by herself on 1st June and Myrtle also caught a fish. Daisy's fish weighed 1lb 12oz and Myrtle's around one pound although Daisy described it somewhat disparagingly as 'a little one'.

Daisy and Myrtle met Marryat for the first time when they, and their parents, had lunch with Halford who was living in another house in the village while work on the mill was being completed. Daisy recorded the meeting:

We go to Mr Halford's to lunch. We meet Mr Marryat. He calls us 'fellows' or 'Johnnies'. He is very funny at dinner. Mr Halford asks me to fill his tobacco pouch for him. When he is out of the room Mr M. takes the pouch, stuffs it with orange peel & one of my gloves.

When Mr H. finds this out he throws the orange peel at Mr M. who nods his head solemnly, so the peel goes over his head.

Later he gave the two girls two Mayflies as did Halford. It was following this and similar incidents that the sisters started to call Marryat 'Aunt Harryat'. Marryat must have been a good friend to the two sisters as he sent them Christmas presents, kept in touch through letters and even gave them advice about keeping pets.

Another example of Marryat's delight at entertaining the young was when he caught a frog on a fly towards the end of August. The poor creature's demise was recorded by Marryat in a mock legal letter:

Know all men by these present that I, G. S. Marryat of the Close Salisbury, did lawfully take and catch with the fly known as the Mayfly in the water known as Moon's Mill pound in the river Kennet, in the parish of Ramsbury one reptile to wit a FROG in the presence of the undersigned this 20th day of August 1894.

The letter was then signed by 'Geo S. Marryat' and witnessed by Flora Kelson and Daisy Field. The artificial Mayfly that Marryat used to catch the frog was hooked into the paper. That fly would surely have been representative of the style and size of Mayfly that he was fishing in the early 1890s. Tony Hayter described the fly as a small wingless version of the Brown Champion which was tied with a body of raffia, ribbed with scarlet thread and gold wire, and a golden pheasant hackle wrapped in front of a ginger cock hackle. It was a variant of a Marryat design that Holland had shown at the Fisheries Exhibition three years earlier.

Although Marryat's last day's fishing at Ramsbury was on 14th June, 1895, he kept in contact with Daisy Field and wrote to her the following year when he was ill in bed. This was the last letter signed Aunt Harryat that Daisy was to receive. Marryat's kindness, letters and presents were remembered by Daisy for the rest of her life. Marryat's eldest daughter Mary Margaret wrote to Daisy after Marryat's death.

Footnote: *Unfortunately, as it has turned out, I did not start work on this book until after the death of Christopher Lloyd whose name, until I started my research, meant nothing to me. Although I contacted the manager of his family home and visited Great Dixter, Daisy Field's youthful diaries and various letters from Marryat had all disappeared, or at least could not be found amongst the masses of papers and other materials that had been horded by the Lloyd family for nearly one hundred years. It will be very interesting to see if they re-appear in years to come in the same way that Marryat's Portmanteau fly-book was lost and then was found (see Chapter 10).*

9

Marryat's Later Years and Death

Although Marryat's life did revolve primarily around fly fishing, he had many other equally compelling interests and passions. Major Turle wrote that he was an accomplished entomologist and 'a past master in gardening' and he wondered how 'his brain could contain so much varied knowledge and yet keep clear and bright'. Marryat was a great lover of nature but he explained to Turle that it was not so much the beauty 'as the mechanism in all things living' that truly interested and intrigued him. As Turle was to write, Marryat would not rest until he had made something out of a subject. Like his collaborator Halford, he had a prodigious enthusiasm for learning all that he could about the many subjects that interested him. Whereas William Senior used the word 'thorough' to describe Halford's approach, I am sure that Marryat's approach, while equally serious, would have been more relaxed and less pedantic, and probably more productive as a result.

Marryat leased what William Greer Turle described as a 'charming old house' in The Close, Salisbury, with a beautiful old garden that was 'a sight to behold':

. . . with sunny walks bounded by high walls, above which towered here and there, amidst the red-brown roofs, the spire of an old church, old even in the days when Salisbury Cathedral was first begun. A kitchen garden full of old gnarled fruit trees, a billowy sea of blossom the first time I saw it, and a glass-house, one of his latest experiments, so full of bright tomatoes that I wondered what he was going to do with them all. And then the flower garden, a map of varied blooms growing side by side in unstudied profusion, for, if I remember rightly, he did not much affect trim bedding-out. Just like himself - unconventional, vigorous, and vivid. He was his own head man, always trying new, and generally successful experiments in a manner enough to addle the brains of any self-respecting or steady-going old-fashioned gardener.

An Indenture dated 13th December, 1884, between the Dean and Chapter of Salisbury Cathedral and Marryat granted him 'a messuage or dwelling house, with gardens, glass house, etc, late in the occupation of Caroline Mary Attwood, deceased, situate on the north of the Close, for a term of seven years'.

He lived there in quite some style it would seem, as in 1891 he had a large household with five servants. Although today the house has only five bedrooms and the adjoining and much older cottage a further two there were probably more in Marryat's day. On the night of the census, 3rd April, 1891, one guest is listed - Frederic M. Halford. It is well known that the two friends often stayed together - at Houghton Mill, at Halford's cottage at Headbourne Worthy up to 1890 (when Halford's lease on the fishing came to an end) and at Ramsbury. While Halford was a regular visitor to Marryat's house in The Close, little is known about how often he stayed there or for how long.

William Senior recounted Marryat's work with the micro-scope and that he 'was an extremely good manipulator, expert at mounting, and in the general work of the instrument'. Turle was of the opinion that Marryat's supple fingers were able to prepare the brain of a bee for study under a microscope as well as any professional. When Sanctuary was writing his stray memories, he noted that 'there are beside me many specimens carefully labelled and signed G.S.M., the mournful souvenirs of delightful hours'. Marryat had a very fine instrument, and friends who came across strange or rare insects would put them on one side for him to study. Once Turle found an unusual 'beast' which he believed had been imported from the Zoological Gardens. Its depredations 'rendered annihilation absolutely necessary'. 'Marryat was greatly interested in the description of its appearance and evil doings, and much regretted that it had not been handed over to him, begging that we look out for another. We never did come across a second and I cannot say I was particularly anxious to do so.'

Latterly Marryat's special study was karyokinesis (the division of a cell nucleus during mitosis). This work saw him become something of an expert at micro-photography. He was already an accomplished photographer and some of his photographs were used to illustrate Halford's books. He was fascinated by the camera and 'he took many trout stream views that would be, to the frequenter of Itchen and Test, priceless'. Red Spinner had a mutual friend who had shown him an album of Marryat's photographs 'produced with a softness and beauty which are rarely surpassed'. In his book *Lines in Pleasant Places*, William Senior wrote: 'Grey had one evening, at the Fly Fishers' Club, been much impressed with a violent tirade from a member about the generally incorrect way in which the ordinary black and white artist illustrates the fisherman in action, and had listened attentively as a group round the fire argued themselves into the conclusion that there was much more to be done with the photographic snapshot in angling than had ever yet been attempted.' Perhaps the Marryat photographs owned by Senior's friend were a step in this direction.

Theodore Gordon, the American correspondent for the *Fishing Gazette* from 1890 and 'the old master of American fly fishing' was an early proponent of dry-fly fishing in the USA and wrote in his column of the *Fishing Gazette* of 11th October, 1913, two years before his death:

What a pity it is that G.S. Marryat did not keep a diary, and that his letters do not seem to have been preserved. The loss to the lovers of the floating fly is very great, as he was not only a wonderful fisher but a man of remarkably attractive personality, judged by the few records we have of him.

* * *

Sanctuary noted that Marryat had 'a presentiment that he would die of consumption' and was always rather careless about taking sufficient precaution against bad weather, particularly when shooting. An example was a January day in 1883 when Marryat and Sanctuary were shooting some snipe moors belonging to Sir Vyell Vyvyan and Mr S. Davey near Helston. They were shooting over gordon setters and as the snipe were few and far between, the party did well to get a bag of ten brace. Although the weather was foul with a strong wind blowing in heavy showers of rain, and there was knee-deep water to wade through, Marryat eventually decided to wear a macintosh but only to keep his companions quiet, but he was very insistent that the rest of the party was properly attired, warm and dry. Sanctuary wrote: 'It was his great characteristic, to be careless of himself and thoughtful for others.' This characteristic was often displayed when shooting as he would regularly volunteer to walk over a particularly nasty piece of ground 'even though it might be the least likely place for a shot, rather than let his friend go without sport'. On the riverbank he would happily spot a fish for a friend to try for, rather than himself.

The idea that catching flu could result in premature death is not as fanciful as it might seem and, indeed, was brought to public attention in the first decade of the twenty-first century in the form of threatened bird and swine-flu pandemics that 'experts' claimed could kill many thousands - if not millions. But figures for the number of people killed in the UK annually by 'normal' outbreaks of winter flu - between 8,000 and 12,000 - are higher than in some major outbreaks. Winter flu usually kills the old and the infirm so when Marryat was taken ill towards the end of January 1896, not one of his friends would have believed that a man who Marston described as an 'exceptionally hard and strong man' would succumb. As that man did, Marston was of the opinion that his death 'ought to make us fear [flu] more than we do'. Halford was to miss much of the early part of the 1896 season because he and other members of his family were stricken down by flu and were staying by the seaside to recuperate. Also Skues declined his first invitation to become a member of the Flyfishers' Club because he had suffered badly from flu and was uncertain as to how long he might live. Marryat had been ill before, in February 1893, and again in the same month two years later with a persistent cough and mild flu. His friend Basil Field announced his last illness to the members of the Flyfishers' Club on Thursday, the day before his death but 'according to a letter that day received, he was not just then in imminent danger'. How wrong it was.

At first Marryat did not take his illness too seriously. After all, he was only fifty-six years old, fit and led a very active life not only fishing but shooting during the winter (Halford wrote that 'Marryat, also a very useful gun, had quite a reputation for arranging partridge drives') and one can assume that he thought that he would shrug-off another bout of flu. Sadly he was wrong and took to his bed at number 20, The Close, Salisbury. This was an unsettling experience for him. His fishing and shooting companion, Major Turle, said of him: 'if ever a man looked likely to enjoy a green old age I should have said that man was Marryat.' Although at one stage Marryat thought that he had got over his illness, he suffered a severe relapse and a major stroke which left him paralysed and unconscious. He was never to regain consciousness. When Field's announcement had stunned into silence the members of the Flyfishers' Club, Marryat was, in fact, lying in bed beyond hope and died the very next day. His unexpected death came as a great shock to Tom Sanctuary and his passing 'left a blank in many hearts outside his own family'.

It was during Halford's tenancy on the Kennet that Marryat succumbed to the severe bout of flu. Halford was to write:

On February 14th, 1896 we all had to deplore the death of George Selwyn Marryat. Even now I cannot write about this sad event, and to all of us at the old mill house it was a dreadful blow.

He had become the dear friend of all there, whether the members of the quadrilateral, their children, their guests, the keepers, every labourer: even, I think, every one of the numerous poachers in the village.

Halford had to miss the early part of the season due to a member of his family succumbing to flu and spent the time beside the sea before going to Ramsbury during the third week of May. He had a very disappointing season, with Marryat's passing ever on his mind and his own health also a problem. Halford did not forget his friendship - and indeed debt to Marryat - and when his book *Dry-Fly Fishing in Theory and Practice* was published three years later in 1899, he arranged for a specially-inscribed copy to be presented to Marryat's widow.

The black cloth upper board was specially stamped *In Memoriam* and the inscription read: 'Mrs G. S. Marryat with the publishers' & author's compliments, April 1899.'

Salisbury Cathedral's Burials' register recorded the burial of George Selwyn Marryat on 18th February. The service was taken by his brother-in-law '[Sir] Talbot HB Baker [Bt.], prebendary or honorary canon'. There is a small memorial plaque set into the grass, close to two cedar trees, in the Cloister Garth inscribed: 'George Selwyn Marryat. Died Feb. 14. 1896. Aged 56.'

Marryat's presentiment that he would die young may have been based on sound evidence. His father was only sixty-four years old when he died in Bath in 1871; his mother had died much earlier in 1860 at Mapperton House; and his uncle Frederick was also but fifty-six years of age when he died.

Marryat's daughter Mary Margaret married the Rev. William Vincent Jephson, vicar of Chilworth, Romsey, on 21st July, 1897. Jephson, the son of a rector, was born at The Rectory, Ayot St Peter, Hertfordshire, in 1874. They had three sons, Selwyn Victor born in Beaminster, Dorset, on 24th May, 1900, Henry James Montague, born on 18th July, 1904, in South Stoneham, Hampshire, and Peter Douglas who was born on 12th September, 1906, also in South Stoneham. They also had two daughters, Margaret L. who was born in Kingsclere in September, 1912, and Elizabeth V. who was born in Christchurch, Hampshire in 1919.

Dorothea Charlotte Edith, Marryat's second daughter, was a boarder at a girls' high school at 36 Frenchgate, Richmond, Yorkshire for the 1901 census and she went on to marry the zoologist Joseph Jackson Lister, from Leytonstone in Essex, in 1911, at Elham, a village in Kent. She inherited her father's interest in science and was to read Biology at Newnham College, Cambridge, where she was one of a number of women geneticists who joined a group of research biologists established by William Bateson. Her research interests were 'The Eye Colour and Sex in Canaries', and 'Variations in *Mirabilis jalapa*'. *Mirabilis jalapa,* which is said to have been exported from the Peruvian Andes in 1540, is known popularly as either the '4 o'clock flower' or the 'marvel of Peru'. The plant is notable because flowers of different colours are found simultaneously on the same plant and individual flowers can exhibit different colours. It also has the ability to change the colour of flower. Dorothea Lister died in 1928, her husband having died on 5th February, 1927.

Of the Marryats's youngest daughter Joan O. Gladstone, there is nothing more to be written. She will, for now, have to remain an enigma.

Marryat's wife Lucy died in September, 1911, at Kingsclere in Hampshire. Between living in Salisbury and her death in Kingsclere, she spent some time back in Shedfield (where she was living before her marriage) and in the census of 1901 her baby grandson Selwyn V. Jephson and his nanny and another Baker niece, Eunice Evelyn, were recorded as staying with her on Botley Road, Shedfield. There were also five servants in the house.

10

Fly Tying and Fly Dressings

In his article 'A Christmas Maunder Anent Grayling', published in *The Field* on 25th December, 1880 (yes, it was published on Christmas Day), Francis wrote that 'we are gradually weeding out the old materials which we used for the bodies of flies formerly, and fur and silk bodies are more and more falling into disuse among first-class trout fishers, being gradually ousted by the introduction of quill, &c'. As Marryat wrote in his letter to the editor in response to the publication of Francis's article, suitable quills needed 'careful selection and careful dyeing' and it was the fact that quills could be dyed or stained to the right colours that made it a practical material to use for the bodies of dry flies. In Francis's opinion the darkening effect of water on silk and fur often resulted in a fly with a body that was too dark to be an accurate imitation of the natural dun. As well as a good quill body producing 'beautiful and accurate effects', Francis liked the material because quill bodies 'hold no water, and float so much better than fur or silk; and as the dry fly is now so very much in favour, that is no small advantage'. It was important that flies were dressed using materials that were likely to float and not absorb water too readily as oil and other treatments for making flies float had yet to be discovered. But Francis did not seem to have thought of using lighter-coloured tying thread and fur dubbing to overcome the darkening when wet. Marryat discussed and argued over many fly tying matters with Francis Francis, whether it was a detail involved in setting wings at the correct angle or a general principle.

Turle described how Marryat had excelled at fly tying for many years but then 'after he had coached Holland in the art' and helped him to perfect his fly-tying skills, he preferred to obtain his flies from him. Marryat had given Turle his first lessons in fly tying and 'a most indefatigable teacher he proved to be'. Tying lessons were held frequently at 7 o'clock in the morning even after the two had been up until the early hours 'yarning'. Marryat often got up even earlier and went 'down to the poultry yard, robbing some poor Andalusian cock of a few hackles, to which he had taken a fancy, and judged would make a killing fly'.

Henry Sinclair Hall, who lived in Clifton, Bristol, was another contemporary whose first tying lessons, apart from what he was able to learn from books, were given by Marryat. Hall had met Marryat in 1876 when fishing Hammond's water at Winchester. To begin with the two were casual acquaintances who used to meet while fishing. In August 1879, Hall met Marryat again on the river and by this time he had started to tie his own flies and was also experimenting with eyed hooks. By 1882 we know that Hall was confident enough in his fly-tying abilities to write a lengthy letter to *The Field* (published on 5th August) on fly tying on eyed hooks. Interestingly he wrote in that letter, 'I puzzled out fly-making myself, without any hints from anyone', although when he wrote his reminiscences of Marryat in the *Fishing Gazette* of 29th February, 1896, he acknowledged that the first lessons he ever had were from Marryat.

Due to common interests, the friendship between Hall and Marryat grew and blossomed over the years. Hall described how Marryat spent 'the hot hours of the afternoon in my rooms tying flies' and chatting amiably. They kept up correspondence and an interchange of ideas relating to fly tying. Hall credited Marryat's eminent practicality and originality in everything that he did and his practical assistance in enabling him to perfect the (then) smallest sizes of eyed fly hooks. Marryat had, in fact, fished with eyed hooks in the early years of the 1870s possibly as much as six years before he met Hall. Hall wrote that this work placed on the then present generation of dry-fly fishermen an obligation to Marryat that they would not be slow to recognise. Hall lived to regret not keeping the letter which he said contained 'a fund of genial wit and humour' and 'original sayings [that] were so smart and original that they will never be forgotten'. Hall remembered how Marryat had described the essentials of a good hook: 'The temper of an angel and the penetration of a prophet, fine enough to be invisible, and strong enough to kill a bull in a ten-acre field.' In the letter to Hall referred to earlier, written in July 1883, Marryat wrote: 'the eyed hooks have done about the same as usual, a few opened and more didn't but a modern philosopher can't ask for miracles & if he does I'll lay the current odds he don't get 'em.'

It seems strange to look back to the introduction of the 'modern' eyed hook (fish hooks with eyes have been found dating back thousands of years) and discover that there was, at the time, much resistance to it. It was possibly the most important development in fly fishing in the Victorian era and without the availability of small eyed hooks made from fine wire, it is arguable that Marryat, Halford and Hall would not have been able to develop dry-fly fishing - often referred to as the dry fly revolution - in the way and to the extent that they did. Sadly Hall became obsessed with the design, development and promotion of eyed hooks. Indeed, he was very upset when his former collaborators in this work, particularly Capt. George Bankhart of Leicester, sought to gain some acknowledgement of their involvement in the development. The dispute between the two raged for some months, particularly in the correspondence columns of the *Fishing Gazette* in 1884, so much so that other correspondents expressed their astonishment at the ill-temper of their exchanges. As David Beazley wrote at some length in *The Flyfishers* (Summer and Winter editions of 1995), the history and the development of the eyed trout hook has many twists and turns and uncertainties. Hall never claimed to have invented the eyed trout hook but he was responsible, along with Bankhart, for developing hooks with a Limerick shape, or bend, and the point offset or snecked. These were marketed by Hutchinsons, a hook-maker in Kendal, as Hall's Snecky-Limerick hooks.

Even as late as 1924 and 1925 Tom Sanctuary was still writing regular letters to the *Fishing Gazette*, some from 1 Crown Terrace, Scarborough. In 1925 he was involved in an exchange of letters on the benefits - or otherwise - of fishing with barbless hooks. His letter, published on 1st August, 1925, attracted a sharp note from the editor: 'I presume Dr Sanctuary is referring to the "Jamison" barbless hooks. In discussing this subject it would be better if correspondents stated exactly what kind of barbless hook they are referring to, and thus avoid confusion.' In his letter Sanctuary stated that he had 'fished since 1860 with barbed hooks alone, and have never even tried the legendary bent pin'. He thought that there were advantages to be gained from using barbless hooks - in the case of the Jamison hook the description as barbless is a slight misnomer as the hook was designed with a kink in the wire to replace the traditional sharp barb - but his one criticism was that the wire used for the smaller sizes was not fine enough. 'If a smaller hook of finer wire were put on the market, it could be dressed more neatly; one hackle instead of two would keep it floating well. At present a single hackle is hardly enough, and two make a fly more bushy than I like.' He finished his letter saying that he was 'sufficiently convinced of the utility of these hooks that I have dressed a good many for friends, and shall be pleased to do so for any readers who would care to experiment'.

One idea of Hall's that did not go anywhere was the use of pike scales as wings. He had produced a black gnat with pike scale wings which Marryat tried. In 1883 Marryat wrote to 'my dear Hall': 'I haven't tried much pike scale. I gave some to Fisher [Major A. T. Fisher] and he got one or two with them, but I don't reckon on them much yet - very nice colours the dyed ones - you omitted that pattern hackle. Try again my son. I shall be sure to come over & see you at Wilton when you come.' The letter ended 'Ta ta, yours, [signed] Geo. S. Marryat'.

Marryat and Sanctuary were responsible for setting up George Holland - who they had 'imported from the north of England and housed' - as a professional fly tyer at 96 Crane Street, Salisbury, 'within ten yards of the river Avon', near to where Marryat lived in The Close. His move was described in the *Fishing Gazette* (11th September, 1886) as being the result of 'the great increase in his business' and his wish 'to be in the heart of the dry-fly district' following correspondence between Holland and Hall who had offered to teach professional fly tyers his method of making and winging dry flies. In a trade directory for 1889 Holland's business was described as 'fishing rod and fishing tackle manufacturer (speciality floating flies and cobweb gut)'. Marryat had benefitted from instruction on tying flies from John Hammond in Winchester and when he had absorbed everything that Hammond knew, he turned his attention to Mrs G. T. Cox of Parchment Street, also in

Winchester. According to Sanctuary, she tied her flies 'with bunchy wings, sometimes split, and from one feather; the two-wing method and the double feather was not then generally practised'. Soon Marryat knew everything that she could teach him and was an acknowledged expert in the art. He had set about learning all he could about dressing flies with the same passion, enthusiasm and single-mindedness that he approached his other passions in life.

Hall, who was a founder member of the Flyfishers' Club, had come across Holland in Failsworth, Manchester and had encouraged him to move south in 1886. Hall had helped Holland with instruction in tying flies, in 1883, in the south country style but Holland was to benefit from frequent visit to his premises by Marryat and Sanctuary and soon had a growing clientele which appreciated his latest designs and dressings of dry flies. (In a letter to *The Field* Hall claimed never to have seen a professional fly dresser at work.) Skues wrote in the summer, 1934 issue of *The Flyfishers' Journal* that 'he also worked out, with the aid of George Selwyn Marryat, the still unsurpassed method of dressing split-winged trout flies on his hooks so that they not only float but cock'.' I think that Skues must have forgotten that in 1923 he had credited Marryat as the sole inventor of the then-new method of winging flies.

Another contemporary who visited Holland in Salisbury was Major Fisher who noted that he had a fly-tying vice with very fine jaws, closed by a sliding ring, which did not get in the way of the tyer's fingers. In his opinion it was much superior to the vice recommended by Halford, but, unfortunately for Fisher, Holland could not remember from where he had acquired it.

'Importing' Holland to Salisbury and setting him up as dresser of chalkstream flies coincided with the start of Marryat's 'most scientific era of fly tying, in which every detail was studied and worked out both by Marryat himself and Holland, under his instructions, with the greatest care'. About this time, Marryat was also bitten 'with the mania of microscopical research' and he and Sanctuary spent hours together 'dissecting and mounting objects, mineral, animal, and vegetable'.

In an article entitled 'The Wheel Full Circle', written in 1929, Skues reminisced about his first days fishing the Itchen 'as a boy at the old school'. When he compared the nymph patterns that he was fishing in the late 1920s, 'dressed to look, not like flies, but like real nymphs', with his memories of the 'flies which old John Hammond sold me as dry flies in 1875', he was struck by the surprising degree of similarity between the patterns. He wrote that only one pattern, the Wickham's Fancy, was dressed as a floating fly while the other eight or ten patterns 'were dressed with slim, tapering, dubbed bodies and with hackles and wings both sloped back from the head in the manner best calculated to give in wet-fly fishing what is called "a good entry", and it was clear to my mind that these flies, though sold as dry flies, were nothing but the old wet flies.' If we dissuade ourselves from thinking that Hammond was simply trying to sell an innocent young tyro some flies that he was anxious to be rid off, then it would seem that there was plenty of scope for Marryat and Halford to produce a range of patterns that could be described as genuine dry flies.

Holland was to move to Winchester, to a shop in Cathedral Square, where Skues used to call in and 'listen to his freely expressed opinions. He was no great respecter of persons except "Alford" and G. S. Marryat'. Sanctuary recorded that Holland was provided with 'a serving-maid as apprentice', a Miss Farley, who carried on tying flies in Wimbledon after Holland had retired in 1912.

It was Marryat's involvement in the development of dry flies that would actually float upright and stay afloat for some time, that was to make dry-fly fishing a practical possibility. Before he and Hall worked out a way of making split-winged trout flies that floated, anglers fished either wet flies, usually across and down, or 'dry' flies that soon absorbed water and were then fished 'wet' or drier after much false casting. Halford suggested that as many as thirty false casts might be needed to dry a fly. Skues did go some way towards confirming this in the article just mentioned when he wrote 'when fished wet with the slim wings drawn tight over the body and the slight hackle drawn under the body' the appearance of such a fly was much more like that of a nymph than a winged fly.

Marryat could be quite cutting in his comments to his fellow anglers on their efforts at fly tying. R. B. Marston had sent Marryat some examples of a fly that he had had tied for him by Ogden of Cheltenham and was known as Marston's Fancy. Marston described it as being a combination of what he considered to be good features in a fly: 'iron-blue wing, hare's flax body, yellow silk head, yellow silk ribbing, silver twist at tail, blue dun whisks, and red cock hackle at shoulder.' It was not until Marston, Marryat and others were fishing with their mutual friend Major Turle on his waters at Newton Stacey, that at lunch Marston, probably to his eternal regret, asked Marryat what he thought of his fly. "Oh, my dear fellow. It is not at all a bad sort of a - of a - common or garden blue dun." This was followed by a roar of laughter 'in which I [Marston] joined, and I never thought much of my fly afterwards.'

Another contemporary who had invited criticism of his fly-tying efforts was Henry Collins. Marryat was clearly a friend of Henry Collins, who was the honorary secretary and treasurer of the Old Hungerford and Wilton Fly Fishing Clubs from 1877 until 1914. The letters passed into the hands of Henry Collins' son, Bernard, who gave permission for them to be published in the *Fly Fisher's Journal,* Autumn 1927 issue. They were published with a brief footnote by J. C. Mottram: 'These two letters are so wanting in ambiguity that to remark upon them could only be distracting.' The first letter was shown as having been written from Shedfield Grange, on a Tuesday, with no date (1882 was written on the envelope) and the second had no address nor date. (As an aside, it is perhaps worth mentioning that I have not discovered a letter that appears to have been written when Marryat was living in Salisbury.)

The first letter, which was accompanied by eighteen flies, tied on size 00 hooks, arranged on a strip of white flannel, was addressed 'My Dear Collins', and read:

I think the same flies do fished sunk as those you fish dry, but I send a few of the best casualty flies for grayling I know; of course you must fish the quills, red, ginger, and blue also.

These run - Indian yellow (A1), brown quill (A1), light blue, black ant, willow (you may have them all tied one size smaller), caperer, silver sedge (little chap with tag), the best fly I know for grayling, a purple bumble (very good at times), crimson tag (A1), little chap (green tinsel), another good bumble and two little blacks. If you can't fiddle 'em with this lot and your own patterns, you oughter, 00's the size, short [shank] for winged flies and long for bumbles. Two flies downstream a yard and a half apart is right with the very finest gut and a long line, let it come round from across the stream, they mostly take it as the flies straighten, so don't hurry the pull out for a fresh cast. Old Francis was in great form, fit and thirsty. Wickham's fancy is a good fly for grayling and a small darkish hare's ear, and sometimes a red ant. That's about all I know.

Yours, Geo. S. Marryat

Thus in a few sentences Marryat passed on some very sound, practical advice. And Walbran would have concurred with the use of very fine gut when fishing for grayling. The fact that in

1882 he was passing on advice about how to fish the down-stream wet-fly would suggest that he had not abandoned the practice entirely since meeting Halford in 1879.

The second, undated letter, was also addressed to 'My Dear Collins' and was a description of good hackles and feathers for fly tying. It was accompanied by examples of feathers which had been attached to the letter 'with slips of gummed paper':

(a) is a good shape and fibre hen hackle; (b) one of yours not nearly so good to my mind; (c) is also very good for tiny midges; (d) is a good shaped and fibred cock hackle for May-fly but wrong colour (it is medium grey); (e) is a right coloured but bad shaped one (it is light ginger). The thing mone can't get is very soft hackle the shape of a good hen's with the shine of a good cock; that's hopeless. A first rate hackle should have shortish thickish fibres and taper very gradually from heel to point when the fibres are drawn back open. (f) Many small hackles look right but are like this gamecock's (g), which is good fibre but bad shape. Now you know all about it.
Yours, Geo. S. Marryat

When this letter was published in the *Journal*, it was accompanied by sketches to show the shapes of the feathers attached to the letter.

In the early years of his work with Halford, the two often talked about the 'want of uniformity in the patterns of artificial flies sold in various shops'. Halford was to write that not only did the sizes, shapes and colours vary from fly dresser to fly dresser, but some fly tyers could not tie to a consistent standard and 'at times a dozen delivered by the same man as the same fly would contain several varieties'. It was the need to be able to buy flies tied consistently to a known pattern that was a driving force behind Halford's wish to publish a book on the methods of dressing flies 'with a considerable number of patterns described and illustrated in colours'. But even then not everyone approved of their ideas of the colours of artificial flies. In his autobiography Halford wrote:

I am reminded of an amusing episode in reference to a very favourable critique which appeared in 1886 on my first book, Floating Flies and How to Dress Them. *After devoting some considerable space to praise generally of the work, it continued in the following terms:*

'*If the question be asked, however, whether the colouring be in all cases adequate to the natural flies of which these are imitations, it seems to us that in a few cases the tints are not sufficiently bright. Thus the duns are suitably subdued in tone, but the red spinner is hardly red enough. At all events, those artificial red spinners which we prefer (tied by Farlow) are many shades more vivid scarlet, and fish seem to run after scarlet, especially a pronounced scarlet, with some avidity.*'

When Marryat read this he fairly exploded with mirth, and summed it up in a few fitting words, saying, "Oh! I see, your critic prefers Farlow's colours to Nature's colours."

As well as being passionate and totally committed to various projects and passions, Marryat was a hard task-master too. One mayfly season around 1886, Marryat and Halford had returned to Houghton Mill after a long, hot and heavy day. They went to bed straight after they had eaten and fell asleep immediately. Poor old Halford was woken after what seemed to him to have been but a short sleep, by Marryat in his pyjamas exhorting him to get up and help him tie some flies. Marryat said: 'What with getting broken, and giving away flies, we have not half a dozen decently dressed May-flies between us.' Halford hauled himself out of bed and into a cold bath, dressed quickly and was down-stairs in the little sitting room before five in the morning. Halford was not in a very good mood and kept showing his temper. But Marryat was in the best of spirits and his enthusi-asm was soon conveyed to Halford who got out their tying vices and all the materials that they would need to tie Mayflies. He also put some maize straw in water to soften it for use as body material. They divided up the work with Marryat winging the flies and Halford completing them.

Marryat passed Halford the first winged hook which Halford placed in his vice and then:

> . . . *fastened in the hackles, carried the silk down to the tail end, working in the whisk, fastened in the gold wire for ribbing, and then forgetting all about the straw body, carried the ribbing hackle down on the whipped hook, and working the wire through the rib-bing hackle, turned the head hackle and completed the fly with the usual whip finish. Then I realised what I had done, and called Marryat's attention to it. He expressed his admiration of the pattern, and in his usual style, suggested as its name, the* ghost, *from the absence of the body.*

They carried on and dressed two dozen flies, half with the cor-rect straw body and the others as 'ghosts'.

When they fished the new accidental variant as well as the proper version, they could detect no lack of enthusiasm from the trout for the 'ghost'. Halford noted that trout seem 'to rise and fasten equally well to both patterns'. They were to have many laughs about this episode over the coming seasons and if pressed for time continued to tie Mayflies without any body. Marryat often 'chaffed' Halford about his short temper that early May morning and as his 'badinage was never of the sort which left a sting, I could laugh at the memory of it with him'.

Halford then went on to point out that cutting the lengths of softened maize straw to the correct size and shape and tying them neatly to the hook all took a considerable amount of time. In due course the use of Ropia grass was adopted for mayfly bodies and Marryat and Halford abandoned the 'ghost' which had, to a degree, offended their taste because it was tied incorrectly.

Joseph Keen wrote many years later of the method 'devised by G. S. Marryat for disposing of the waste fibre at the roots of the wings'. He felt that it would be appreciated by readers who were as ham-fisted as the author. For him the problem was cutting away cleanly the ends of the feathers used for wings; if not trimmed away cleanly, the stalks could foul the eye of a hook. Once the wings had been tied in place in the usual way, the waste ends were separated and then turned back to lie alongside the hook shank and tied down. The waste ends could then be trimmed more easily and blended smoothly into the body. This method also added security as the wings could not be pulled out.

There are many often tantalisingly brief references in contemporary books to fly patterns devised by Marryat. At one time it seemed that there were but two patterns that had survived, the Little Marryat and Marryat's Ibis Tag. Senior wrote at the time of Marryat's death that 'There is one fly - the Little Marryat - which bears his name'. Major A. T. Fisher, in *Rod and River or Fly-Fishing for Salmon, Trout and Grayling*, included the dressing for the Little Marryat. In *Dry-Fly Fishing, Theory and Practice*, Halford noted that Marryat had developed a very effective pattern - using Gutta Percha tissue for the body - that could be used to catch tailing trout. 'A really good imitation of the freshwater shrimp might at times be successful in basketing an old trout here and there, and such an imitation has been dressed by my good friend Marryat, who has shown it to me. Both of us, however, have solemnly sworn never to reveal the secret of it'. He then went on to add that it was the only artificial fly which either of them had refused to give to a fellow angler and that as neither of them ever used it, they went so far as to refuse to carry it in their fly boxes, Halford asked his readers not to think that his refusal to pass-on the details of the pattern was motivated by selfishness. Another Marryat pattern referred to by Halford was 'a most efficacious' nymph pattern:

. . . dressed without wings, with Egyptian goose hackle, body of the palest buff, maize-coloured floss silk, ribbed with a strand of peacock's herl, which is of pale cinnamon colour at the root. The pale portion of the herl is worked at the shoulders so as to show about three turns of the dark metallic bronze at the tail of the body, which fairly represents the darker markings on this portion of the natural fly. The tail is of brown mallard, or gallina, dyed to this colour. It is, however, a very difficult fly to dress, owing to the stubborn nature of the stem of the Egyptian goose hackle.

Marryat was a much more pragmatic fly fisherman than Halford and would, one might speculate, had he not worked so closely with Halford on developing dry-fly fishing and suitable flies, have been happy to continue to fish artificial nymphs to nymphing fish, or when fish were not feeding on the surface. Although it was thought at this time that it was impossible to fish an artificial nymph in an effective manner, in *The Dry-Fly Man's Handbook*, Halford maintained that it was possible that 'any fly-dresser who sets his mind to it' can dress an effective nymphal imitation very easily. He then went on to describe how many years ago he and Marryat had 'dressed most effective patterns to represent the nymphs of duns and mayflies'. In his book *Nymph Fishing For Chalk Stream Trout*, Skues maintained that he had 'grounds for knowing that the date when Marryat was dressing artificial nymphs was before 1883'. This was based on the fact that Marryat had given a friend of Skues, the Rev. E. R. J. Nicolls, some artificial nymphs when Nicolls was fishing, during the tenancy of Marryat and Francis, the same length of the Itchen that Irwin Cox took over at the beginning of 1883. Marryat and Halford tied a few fibres from a black feather at the head of the pattern, then a quill body of the same colour as the natural nymph, a short, sparse hackle, and a short tail of gallina dyed to the correct colour. Halford explained how they tied the fly: 'When the body material had been tied in the fibres of black feathers were bent down into a shallow loop to represent the wing cases of the natural nymph, the hackle was then turned, and the fly finished at the head.' Although these artificials proved to be successful and Marryat and Halford caught fish with them, and in spite of the fact that 'It must not, however, be forgotten that in poor Marryat's own terse words, "while floating food is *caviare*, sunk or mid-water food is *beef* to the fish"'. Halford was adamant that neither of them should fish with them. This was for two reasons. The first was that these artificial flies were 'essentially wet-flies, and the use of them on waters reserved for the dry fly only, constituted a breach of the ethics of the dry fly'. I don't think that many anglers today would disagree with this reason but it makes questionable the sense of limiting anglers to the dry fly only. Halford maintained that no one should try for a bulging fish in a dry-fly only river. The second reason that Halford promulgated for not fishing with artificial nymphs was that too many fish hooked were then lost - a number that 'was out of all proportion to the total bag' - and this resulted in those fish becoming 'inordinately shy and unapproachable'.

Halford was never as good a fisherman as Marryat and so it is not surprising that he did not set the hook into that many trout, using an artificial and method that he could not accept as being true fly fishing. (Skues was also critical of Halford's ability to catch fish and the coarseness of some of the tackle that he used.) But was Halford right that Marryat also failed to hook and catch trout using nymphs? The nearest that we can get to an answer to this question is the two paragraphs that Halford wrote on the 'danger of striking fish taking Mayfly too quickly'. Marryat and Halford were walking along the river bank at about six o'clock one evening when they saw 'a huge trout come to the surface and take a spent gnat' just upstream from a railway bridge. Marryat would not try for it so Halford did, with a spent gnat. The fish rose very deliberately but Halford struck too quickly and, as he admitted, probably 'far too violently'. He did not touch the fish and Marryat exclaimed: "You silly old chump, you pulled the fly away before it could take it." Fortunately for a chastened Halford, the fish soon started to rise again. It was now Marryat's turn to show Halford how to catch it. So Marryat tied on a spent gnat and placed it accurately within inches of where the fish was rising. 'Again it came up quite slowly. Marryat struck and never touched it. "Shall I repeat the 'silly old chump' sentence?" Oh! That trout never rose again that day.'

Later in *Dry-Fly Fishing, Theory and Practice* we are appraised of the spent gnat pattern devised by Marryat, 'the result of life-long study'. The dressing that he gives is for the wings, which are tied horizontally and at right-angles to the hook shank, to be made from four transparent blue Andalusian grizzled cock hackle points; the body was white floss silk ribbed with a cinnamon-ended strand of peacock; whisks or tails of brown mallard or gallina which should be dyed a very dark brown that is nearly black; a grey partridge hackle at the shoulder and a badger cock hackle 'carried down the body from the shoulder to the tail end'.

Little Marryat

Hook : 00
Tail : Pale buff Cochin cock hackle fibres (or pale olive gallina)
Body : Fur from the flank of an Australian opossum
Hackle : Pale buff Cochin cock hackle
Wings : Youngest and palest starling, tied quite upright

The Little Marryat was number fourteen in Halford's 'The Hundred Best Patterns of Floating Flies' as published in Baily's *Magazine of Sports and Pastimes,* and number fifteen was the Quill Marryat which Halford described as his improvement on the Little Marryat.

Quill Marryat

Hook : 00
Tail : Pale buff Cochin cock hackle fibres
Body : A strand of peacock eye slightly bleached in hydrogen
   peroxide, until it is the *café au lait* colour of opossum fur
Hackle : Pale buff Cochin cock hackle
Wings : Youngest and palest starling, tied quite upright

Marryat's Ibis Tag

Hook : No 0, Kendal scale
Tag : Scarlet Ibis feather
Body : A strand of Macaw tail feather, stripped, wrapped
carefully to show alternate rings of blue and yellow
Hackle : Blood red cock hackle

Walbran described this as 'One of Mr Marryatt's *(sic)* patterns, and a great favourite in south country chalkstreams; it kills equally well elsewhere, and there is no doubt whatever that the brilliant scarlet of the natural feather long outlives that of either wool or silk floss'. In *Dry-Fly Fishing*, Halford referred to this pattern as being 'the improved pattern of that fly [the red tag] invented by Mr Marryat'. He described how the single strand of Macaw tail feather, which is 'a brilliant metallic blue on one side, and a bright yellow on the other', when 'rolled on to form the body, it has the appearance of being a yellow ground with a fine blue rib running up it'.

In *Floating Flies and How to Dress Them,* Halford attributed the following dressings to Marryat.

Hackled Red Spinner

Hook : 0 or 00
Whisk : Pale cream colour
Body : Peacock or adjutant* quill dyed in No. IX, ribbed with fine gold wire
Hackle : Honey dun cock over three or four turns of black ostrich at shoulder

Halford published another dressing for this fly that he described as 'Mr Marryat's well-known pattern'. It has wings and omits the black ostrich at the shoulder.

Hook : 0, 00 or 000
Whisks : From a pale cream-coloured Dorking cock hackle
Body : Peacock or adjutant quill dyed in No. IX and ribbed with fine gold wire
Wings : Honey dun cock-hackle points
Hackle : Black butted red game cock

*A quill from an adjutant stork. The bird got its name because of its similarity to a military adjutant who stands to attention while his superiors file in. The adjutant will stand motionless for hours at a time in its tropical home in India and south-eastern Asia. It is the largest of the storks.

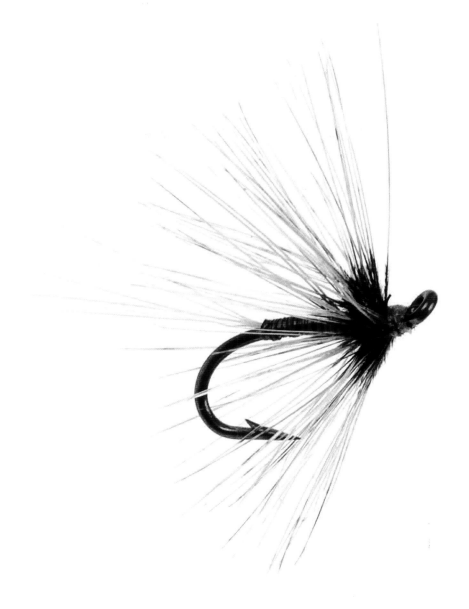

Brown Badger

Hook : 0 or 00
Whisk : Pale cream colour
Body : Peacock quill dyed in No. 1X
Hackle : Badger cock

Needle Brown

Hook : 00 long
Tag : Very pale primrose floss silk
Body : Orange tying silk
Hackle : Honey dun cock

'Mr Marryat's imitation of the female 'Needle Brown', the tag representing the eggs.'

Corkscrew

Hook : 1, 0 or 00
Body : The quill of a red-brown partridge tail-feather from which the plume has been entirely cut away with scissors [And flattened by drawing it backwards and forwards between the thumb nail and forefinger.]
Hackle : Brown ginger cock

Halford wrote: 'In small streams or coloured water it is considered irresistible by Mr Marryat, to whose inventive genius this pattern is due.'

Hook : 000
Body : Strand of cock golden pheasant tail, or brown turkey tail
Wings : Palest starling
Hackle : Two cock starling hackles

The Rev. Patrick Smythe's called this in his diary, 'a little Curse of poor old Marryat's pattern' (entry for 18th May, 1896, *The Diary of an All-Round Angler*). This pattern was number 57 in Halford's 'The Hundred Best Patterns of Floating Flies' as published in Baily's *Magazine of Sports and Pastimes*.

Hook : 3-long, or smaller
Body : White floss silk ribbed with a
  cinnamon-ended strand of peacock
Whisks (or tail) : Brown mallard or gallina,
  dyed a very dark brown that is nearly black
Wings : Four transparent blue Andalusian
  grizzled cock hackle points, tied horizontally
  and at right-angles to the hook shank
Hackle : Grey partridge hackle at the shoulder,
  and a badger cock hackle carried down the
  body from the shoulder to the tail end

There is a variation of the dressing for 'The old
standard pattern of spent gnat worked out by
Marryat' which was:

*. . . wings of four dark grizzled blue dun cock hack-
les set on horizontally; a grey partridge hackle at head,
a badger cock hackle at shoulder, and another badger
cock hackle ribbing the body which is of condor, dark
at the point and white at the root, the white part at
shoulder and two or three turns of the dark part of the quill at the
tail end of the body; a fine silver wire ribs the body and fastens
securely each turn of the ribbing hackle; the whisk is of gallina dyed
a very dark brown, and the hook is No. 3 long.*

Mayfly Nymph

Tail : Brown mallard, or gallina, dyed to this colour

Body : Palest buff, maize-coloured floss silk, ribbed with a strand of peacock's herl, pale cinnamon colour at the root.

Thorax : Pale portion of the herl at the shoulders to show about three turns of the dark metallic bronze at the tail of the body

Hackle : Egyptian goose

Grannom Nymph

Hook : 1 or 2
Body : Peacock or condor quill dyed in Crawshaw's Grannom
  Green
Wing : A small piece of the point of a brown partridge hackle
Hackle : A rusty dun cock hackle

This dressing was in Halford's 'The Hundred Best Patterns of
Floating Flies' as published in Baily's *Magazine of Sports and
Pastimes.* Although Halford did not attribute it directly to
Marryat, it seems unlikely that it was not one of his patterns.

Tying the wings at right-angle to the shank of the hook was a real Marryat innovation that has stood the test of time as this is the very same method that is still used to tie spent fly patterns. He recommended that the fly be tied on a hook no larger than '3-long' and even smaller for very shy fish. In *The Dry-Fly Man's Handbook*, Halford wrote:

The old standard pattern of the spent gnat worked out by Marryat is dressed with wings of dark grizzled blue dun cock hackle set on horizontally; a grey partridge hackle at head, a badger cock hackle ribbing the body which is of condor, dark at the point and white at the root, the white part at shoulder and two or three turns of the dark part of the quill at the tail end of the body, a fine silver wire ribs the body and fastens securely each turn of the ribbing hackle; the whisk is gallina dyed a very dark brown, and the hook is a No. 3 long.

In 1895 Halford fished the Kennet only once before the mayfly started to hatch on 31st May. It was a moderate hatch, for the time, that lasted until 13th June. Nearly all the fish that Halford caught were on 'Marryat's pattern of the spent gnat'. Halford's new patterns, Nos 5 and 6, which represented the male and female spent gnat, 'were worked out with the greatest care, and I firmly believe that, had he been spared to see them, my dear friend Marryat would have been the first to admit that they were more lifelike and nearer to nature than his own standard pattern'. He also felt that Marryat would have approved of his plan of representing both sexes instead of just the female which Marryat's pattern represented.

The use of condor feathers for fly tying can be attributed to Hall who had been keeping an eye on a bird in Clifton Zoo for many years and was for an equally long time probably the sole supplier of these feathers to fly dressers, both professional and amateur. After the bird eventually died Hall wrote about its demise in *The Field*, in 1910, in an article entitled 'A Bird Famous in The Annals of Fly Dressing'.

The male condor in the Clifton Zoological Gardens died but a short time ago. His exact age was not known, but he was the oldest inhabitant of the gardens; I have good reason for supposing he was not less than thirty-five years old, and may even have been several years older. It is probable that hundreds of anglers have had an unconscious interest in this bird, and it is equally probable that at the present time there are not half a dozen readers of The Field *who know that the Clifton condor has been responsible for the capture of many thousands of trout and grayling. In the belief that the subject may be of some interest to fly fishers, I venture to give the following account.*

About thirty years ago my children, who were often in the Zoological Gardens, used to bring me feathers to add to my stock of fly-making materials. One day they brought me one of the large outer wing feathers of the condor. The best of these feathers are of a beautiful creamy grey tint, others vary in shade from almost pure white to a brownish slate, and they are so large that a single feather will furnish an amateur with enough strands to last a lifetime. It occurred to me at once that, when stripped of the flue, the strands would provide a 'quill' which could be dyed so as to imitate successfully almost any kind of body for duns and flies of that class. After some experiments, I introduced the new material to several of my friends, who at once recognised the value of the discovery. The letters I received in this connection from the late Francis Francis and G. S. Marryat are so characteristic of the writers that perhaps I may be permitted to give some quotations. The first is from my dear old friend Marryat, the best and most unselfish sportsman, and at the same time the most genial angling compan-

ion that I have ever met. *All who knew him will recognise his racy, amusing, unconventional style. The letter is dated Dec. 30, 1882, and, without a word of preamble of any kind, bursts into the following quaint mixture of humour and nonsense:*

'Oh, my! skin the first condor you shoot about Clifton entire, and roast the carcase for yourself and your family. As for me and my, family, we will be content with the feathers. Are you quite sure that you haven't been entertaining (and plucking) an angel unawares in the Zoo? What do you think I should say if I saw the lot you've kept for yourself? Oh, you did, you know. I know by that tip you tore from your heart and sent among the rest. I calculate I can tie 24,805,923 flies with what I've got, so I won't be rough upon you. Do you feel to want any feathers I've got? If so, give it a name, and I'll try to send them . . . Long life to you and your condor; tell the keeper the sooner that bird is 'conned o'er' again, the better.'

The letter from Francis Francis bears date Jan. 7, 1883. After some remarks about some eyed hooks which I had sent along with the feathers, he says: 'As regards condor, he looks fine, and is jam for olives, but that dark-winged one is not solved yet. The enclosed strand which I pick out is exactly the colour of the beast just after he is batched, and when the trout are mostly mad on him; but it wants a darker clip for the head and tail, and that is not difficult to do, I fancy . . . The condor certainly is a find, and I have an idea that it might even do for mayfly.'

Francis followed this up with a visit to Regent's Park, where he discovered that there was no condor old enough to supply the right feathers. These birds are a long time in arriving at adult plumage, and until they have reached maturity their feathers are too dark to be of any use as far as the bodies of delicate duns are concerned, And so it happened that for some years the Clifton condor was the only bird in England known to be capable of supplying the needs of anglers. Practically, I have had the monopoly of all the feathers moulted, and I have sent them here, there, and everywhere to my

*angling friends, as well as to one or two professionals specially inter-
ested in dry fly work. In particular, I may mention Mr George
Holland, now of Kingston-on-Thames, and Miss A. Farley, of
Wimbledon.*

*At the time I am speaking of, small eyed hooks for trout flies had
only been in vogue a short time, and Holland (who was then living
at Failsworth, near Manchester, and whom I never saw until there
had been an exchange between us of something like a hundred letters) did a great deal to popularise their use by his clever handiwork.
He was the first professional who recognised that eyed hooks had come
to stay, and that if floating flies on these hooks were to satisfy the
exacting demands of dry-fly fishermen some modification of time-
honoured, but mistaken, methods of tying were necessary. It is a safe
venture to say that in the early eighties Holland himself must have
tied flies which can only be numbered by thousands, and as his business was almost confined to floating flies, a very large proportion of
these were made with condor 'quill' supplied by myself.*

*Condor feathers are not now so difficult to procure as they were
formerly. A year or two ago I noticed many (though not the best
specimens) displayed in milliners' shops, and of late years I have
not myself collected so many feathers for distribution as I used to do.
But the fact remains that the noble bird, whose loss we deplore
locally, and which I have myself known for more than thirty years,
was at one time the sole provider of the material for a valuable
class of flies, which were perhaps being unconsciously used by scores
of readers of* The Field *when in quest of trout and grayling.*

The Yellow May Dun was another fly of the chalkstreams that
Marryat and Halford imitated although neither ever caught a
sizeable fish with it. Their pattern was tied with upright, hackle
point wings dyed sulphur yellow, a hackle and tails dyed green-
ish yellow and a quill body that was dyed yet another shade,
this time lemon yellow. The number of different dyes used

shows the painstaking lengths to which the two went in their quest for 'perfect imitation'. For dyeing green drake wings, Halford published 'Mr Marryat's recipe' as follows:

Soak the feathers for at least twenty-four hours in solution of alum, then rinse out in cold water; make a decoction of a handful of outside onion-leaves to a pint of boiling water. Dye the feathers in this until they are a distinctly orange olive tint, wash out thoroughly, and then dye in a solution of a quart of boiling water to a small quantity of Judson's 'slate', a few drops of Stevens' Blue Black ink, and two or three grains of Crawshaw's 'green'. If the colour produced is in any way bright it is wrong, and the feathers must be taken out just as the latter dye is driving off the former. By the use of this recipe, the green drake wings are dyed of the subdued blue green tint of the natural fly.

In *Modern Development of the Dry Fly* Halford referred to Marryat's recommendation of gallina which he thought 'in my humble opinion is to-day the only feather fit for making the whisk of a floating fly; no other feather is at once so tough, stands so much use, and is in substance and appearance so similar to the setae of the natural insect'.

As well as developing his method for tying split-wing dry flies, Marryat also invented 'a pair of long bull-dog pliers' which were made by Messrs Weiss, surgical instrument makers on the Strand, London, and who held the pattern. These were used by Marryat, Halford and others no doubt, for holding together two pairs of feathers (two from the left wing and two from the right wing of a bird) so that the projecting sections could be detached as a set of wings. When one set of wings had been removed, the pliers were opened and the feathers moved beyond the point to make another set of wings. Halford wrote: 'In this way sufficient feathers can be arranged at one time to make six or eight sets of wings.' The invention was dated to 1882 by Skues who was lent correspondence between Marryat and Hall and the invention was written about in a letter posted on 25th November of that year. Skues also remembered in later years how he had seen girls in George Holland's tying room 'winging hooks with extra-ordinary speed' using Marryat's design of winging pliers. Marryat wrote of 'a new winging for eyed hooks' which he described as 'quicker than the old' and, in his opinion better too, using 'a pair of long jawed bulldog forceps', rather than pliers. At the end of the letter he admitted that he had tied only half a dozen flies in the way that he had described.

Details of this invention obviously found their way to America as Theodore Gordon wrote in his column of 9th May, 1914: 'Do you remember the little "Bulldog" pliers invented by G. S. Marryat many years ago? They were designed to hold the entire plumes from two or four starling wings (right and left) when winging flies. I find these pliers a convenience for holding small things or tying silk.'

Halford wrote about the method that he used to make dubbed fly bodies, using a dubbing rope or brush. He hung a short length of tying silk, in a loop, over a nail driven into the edge of his tying table. He then applied the dubbing material to one of the strands and then locked it in place with the other strand. By spinning together the two lengths of thread, he made a hackle brush which he then used to produce a dubbed fly body. But was Halford the actual developer of this technique? W. H. Lawrie suggested in his book *All-Fur Flies and How to Dress Them*, that Marryat was responsible for this idea. Lawrie wrote: 'In the early notes of that undoubted authority, the late G. E. M. Skues, its invention is ascribed to Marryat.' Lawrie then quoted an extract from Skues so-far unpublished autobiography (*Trivialities of a Long Life*) in support of his assertion. Skues described 'Captain (*sic*) Marryat's Method' thus:

Take a piece of fine sewing silk and tie a knot at one end. Stick a pin between the strands into your table. About 3 inches from the pin untwist the silk so that the strands stand wide open - enough to admit your placing a small quantity of fur-fibres or mohair between the strands of silk. Having done so, twist the silk and allow the fur-fibres or mohair to spin like a wire brush, pulling out the superfluous fibres as you twist.

It is interesting for fly tyers in the twenty-first century to note that Marryat persuaded Halford to wrap the silk tying thread in the 'wrong' or 'left-handed' direction, that is towards the tyer rather than away, at the start of his fly-tying career. This is a practice that was never popular and did not last although Halford wrote some years later, 'I advise all who can to follow his precedent, because it certainly seems more convenient, and at each lap, when drawing the silk taut, the right hand is below the work, quite clear of it, and the fly in process of dressing is easily seen'. He passed-on this advice in 1910 when *Modern Development of the Dry Fly* was published.

* * *

When Marryat died, one of his fly books - known as 'the Portmanteau' by his friends - passed into the hands of Basil Field and when he, Field, died, in 1908, it found its way into the ownership of another member of the Flyfishers' Club, James Rolt KC, who gave it to the Club in 1934. Hall related to Skues how Marryat had told him, in jest, that 'I can just lay this down on the bank till the fish crowd around and I can pick the big ones, saying, "Shoo, fish, you are only 2lb" to the smaller ones'. Rolt allowed Skues to study it and he wrote a lengthy article which was published in the *Fly-Fishers' Club Journal*, Nos 45 and 46, Spring and Summer issues of 1923. The Portmanteau contained what Skues considered to be some of the first examples of the Little Marryat 'but the body appears to be hare's poll' rather than fur from the flank of an Australian opossum, or a peacock quill bleached in dioxide of hydrogen to a *café au lait* shade. These must be Quill Marryats. (A contemporary fly tyer who also used opossum fur was R. S. Austin who is best-known for the fly that Skues named Tup's Indispensable, although that fly did not include opossum. He tied a light olive dun that did include pale fawn-coloured opossum, a pale evening dun, and various other dun patterns that all used opossum fur in dressing the bodies. Who introduced the fur to Austin? Was it Marryat who might have brought some back from Australia, or was it Francis Francis who had been presented with an opossum rug? Sadly we will probably never find out.)

According to Skues with but one exception every one of the hundreds of flies contained by the fly book (we know from Red Spinner's comments earlier that both Marryat and Halford were in the habit of carrying large quantities of flies with them when they were fishing) were tied on up-eyed hooks as devised by Hall, namely Snecky Limericks. The significance of this statement is that it enabled Skues to date the flies to between the autumn of 1879 - the year these hooks were first available - and Marryat's death in 1896, and probably as early as 1883. As well as using the style and pattern of hook to date the flies, Skues noted that, with few exceptions, they were lightly dressed with single wings made from one slip from a wing and doubled, rather than Marryat's later method using matching slips to make double wings. These flies had not been tied commercially and Skues attributed them to Marryat and his friends. Indeed, correspondence with Tom Sanctuary confirmed that it was very likely that Sanctuary had tied many of them as he claimed to have dressed hundreds of flies for his very close friend. Another interesting deduction that Skues made was that after the publication of Halford's book *Floating Flies and How to Dress Them* in 1886, Marryat must have either given up dressing his own flies or had stopped using this fly book. Had he not read Major Turle's comments on how Marryat virtually gave up tying his own flies once he had taught Holland how to tie flies suitable for the southern chalkstreams? A contemporary review of *Floating Flies and How to Dress Them* referred to Marryat's improved ways of tying a wide range of different flies, including ones with detached bodies, being evident in the patterns in the book.

Skues seemed to have been surprised at the large size of many of the flies, tied as they were on hooks no smaller than No. 0, often with long shanks, and some as large as No. 2 long. Hall told Skues that flies for chalkstreams in the 1870s and 1880s were tied very much bigger then. Writing in the early years of the nxt century Russell quoted Charles Kingsley as admitting 'that on some chalk-streams "midges" were needed, and that on the Itchen at Winchester hardly any flies but small ones were used after the green-drake was off. But the Winchester fishers confessed that they lost three good fish out of four on their very small flies.'

The book - which measures ten inches long, five inches wide and some two inches thick - was made from pigskin with a large pocket at each end and twelve parchment divisions that were intended for storing flies tied to gut; there were extra parchment pockets for casts. There were also ten sheets of flannel, with hemmed edges, attached by brass clips to each sheet of fly pockets. Amongst an assortment of casts and other angling paraphernalia in one of the pockets was a parchment container with three pockets, two of which held split shot. The first sheet of flannel held ninety flies, Skues did not count the number on the second sheet, the third 150, then 127, 127, 95, 119 and then 149. The last parchment sheet had two flannel pads but Skues did not give a figure for the numbers of flies on them. One of the sheets, or pads, holds early examples of the best-known of Marryat's artificial flies, the Little Marryat.

Skues' overall feelings about the fly book were that it contained flies much more suited to fishing, probably wet, on the rough water more typical of North Country streams than the Hampshire chalkstreams, based on what he described as 'the enormous predominance of patterns better calculated to fish wet than dry' and he then surmised that Marryat had ceased to use it and the flies it contained and perhaps towards the end of his life had 'carried a fly box for chalkstreams and used the book for the rough water fishing of other rivers'. From an even greater distance, this does not seem to be unlikely. Marryat did fish for grayling in Derbyshire, had fished the Eden (Hall had told Skues that Marryat had a friend with water on the Eden) and had even experimented - for a short while with Halford no less - with nymphs. As Terry Griffiths noted more recently, the portmanteau holds large numbers of March Browns 'a fly more commonly associated with the streams and rivers of the North and West Country' rather than the Hampshire chalkstreams. As the fly book contained packets of split shot one can but assume that he used them to weight his cast to fish his wet flies - or nymphs? - at some depth below the surface. Skues described some of the flies as 'quite nymphal in type'. Towards the end of the article Skues wrote:

Looking back over the collection one cannot help being impressed with the enormous predominance of patterns better calculated to fish wet than dry, and it seems impossible to doubt that at one stage of his angling career, and that not much separated from the period of Marryat's collaboration with Halford, indeed overlapping more or less, the great man must have been content either on chalkstreams or on other waters to fish what Mr Aflalo called 'as wet as Niagara'.

This was quite true as Sanctuary confirmed that Marryat did not start dry-fly fishing until his return from Australia, and Skues himself knew that many of the flies sold as dry flies were remarkably similar to those sold as wet flies, if they were not actually identical.

W. H. Lawrie held that Marryat 'was [also] an accomplished wet-fly fisher if the evidence of his fly-book [the famous 'portmanteau'] held any significance'.

As the Grannom was a fly of such importance to the Victorian angler it seems strange that Marryat did not develop an artificial. A contemporary dressing for the Grannam (*sic*) or Green Tail was published in 1860 in Henry Wade's book *Rod-Fishing in Clear Waters by Fly, Minnow, and Worm*:

Wings, to lie flat, of the clouded feather of the partridge, but the best is from the hen pheasant; body, the dark fur of the hare's ear mixed with a little blue mole's fur; the tail, from the green herl of the eye of a peacock's feather, or a small piece of green wax, of the size of a pin's head, is the best representation of nature; legs, a yellow grizzle or pale ginger hackle. With a woodcock's feather over the same body it may be dressed as a hackled-fly, but it does not answer so well. I have known a piece of grass used for the tail, and a nice dish of trout taken with it. Limerick hook, No. 2.

The Portmanteau was borrowed by a member of the Flyfishers' Club in the mid-1970s and the Club lost track of it for a while. The borrower died in 2003 and although the Club's then librarian John Morgan, wrote to his widow, he had no response. In due course a copy of the borrower's will and details of the executors were obtained. Morgan contacted an executor who was, eventually, able to confirm that he was in possession of the fly-book and much to everyone's relief, the fly-book was re-claimed by the Club and is now back in the Club's ownership and safe-keeping.

In his 2009 article for *The Flyfishers,* 'The Portmanteau of George Selwyn Marryat', Terry Griffiths was able to cast some interesting light on the way that Marryat - and probably Sanctuary as well - tied his flies. He wrote: 'In the Portmanteau, hackles are tied as per wet-fly technique and so would create a footprint in the surface film, or may be fished wet in what we nowadays call an emerger style, a most killing manner of presentation.' He also noted that although the flies were tied on some of the first examples of eyed hooks, they had been tied in a very similar style to how gut-tied flies were tied on blind hooks. 'The dry flies are tied as a variation of the wet fly, e.g. using cock hackle rather than hen, and are typically larger than Halford prescribed.' Griffiths described how most of the flies had been tied with the hackle 'added into the tying before the wing is applied as is normal with wet patterns, the wing being the last item to be applied. What changes here is that the wing is tied in and brought into the upright (or near) position, and then the hackle is wrapped behind the upright wing to bolster it. There are one or two examples where the hackle does cross in front of the wing for only one turn, but may be a matter of neatness rather than design.' He felt that the flies in the book represented 'a transitional stage' from the old style of tying flies on blind hooks to developing a method of tying on the then-new eyed hooks. This might account for what Griffiths describes as 'a vast range of tyings throughout the wallet, varying to some small dgree in the manner of tying, very much in keeping with the work of a keen amateur fly-tyer'. There are no split-wing dry flies and the wings of the dry flies were tied using a single strip of quill. These rolled wings were tied unsplit.

11

Final Words

Following Marryat's death on 14th February, 1896
the tributes on the following pages were published in
the angling press. What better way to end this book than
to reproduce them here? Both poems were also published
in *The Wykehamist* of 30th March, 1896,
with the following introduction:

George Selwyn Marryat, Wykhamici Olim Alumni,
Viri Praeclari Ingenii, Et Piscatorum Facile Principis;
Qui Obit Feb. 14, 1896, Et In Claustris Ecclesie
Cathedralis Apud Sarum Sepultus Est.

The Fishing Gazette, 14th March, 1896

A WREATH FOR
GEORGE SELWYN MARRYAT'S TOMB

COTSWOLD ISISYS, AUTHOR OF 'LYRA PISCATORIA', LAUREATE OF THE F.F.C.

When Sarum lifts her lofty spire
Above green lawns in beauty spread
There falls a gloom of sorrow dire
Sad Avon mourns her lover dead!
'No more,' she sighs, 'that kindly eye
That often look'd in love on me,
Nor heedless ever passed me by,
Shall I again rejoicing see!'
Nor all alone doth Avon mourn,
Two sister nymphs in equal woe
Are weeping each beside her urn,
Where Test and Itchen from them flow.
Of both, his form had seem'd a part,
For on their breasts, with pliant wand,
In gentle play of winsome art,
He often laid a lover's hand.
What hand with such grace could cast
Or lightlier lay the mimic fly?
Or make its dry wings flutter past
So truly, trout or grayling's eye?
What generous envy fill'd their breast
Who saw him ply that wond'rous wand;
Or heard him tell with modest zest
His tales of sport in many a land!
Less poet than mechanic he;

Rarely his soul could beauty stir;
Not Nature's Artist did he see,
So much as her Artificer.*
Yet no mechanic soul was his;
They say who felt his friendship's flame;
But one aglow with sympathies
That self completely overcame.
Our brotherhood with grief sincere,
This tribute to their Prince would pay,
And drop o'er Marryat's tomb a tear
As on it this sad wreath they lay.

* 'Nothing was too small or great for his observation; a true lover of Nature, though he was always careful to explain (why, I know not) that it was not the beauty so much as the wonderful mechanism in all things living that fascinated him.'
MAJOR W.G. TURLE, *F.G.*, FEB. 29.

Max Walbran added a footnote: 'This was absolutely the case. Mr Marryat told me the same thing as we wandered together on the banks of the Test, and yet in the garden behind his house at Salisbury the flower beds were one mass of rich colours. But Marryat was always a very curious man to comprehend at any time.'

The Fishing Gazette, 21st March, 1896

In Memoriam
GEORGE SELWYN MARRYAT
Piscatorum facile principis.

T. SANCTUARY, M.D. LONDON, MARCH 14, 1896

Sleep, cherished friend, secure from storm and wind;
Thy life well acted, and thy past well played!
Where could a Selwyn fairer haven find
Than 'neath the sacred spire in cloistered shade?

Snatched from our hearts, he journeys forth alone,
With keener gaze than mortal powers admit.
At last he lifts the veil from the Unknown,
And solves the secrets of the Infinite.

Shrewd humour, caustic wit: to chosen friend
A friend always: than brother more to me.
Why to a life like his such early end?
Yet deeds, not years, count immortality.

No more for him the bleating snipe shall twist
Beneath the slopes of wind-swept Eggardon;*
Nor woodcock flushed from out the purple mist,
On Cornish moors or woods of Mapperton.*

And ne'er again, where Avon's waters glide,
Shall watchful keeper hear his footsteps pass;
Nor Itchen's wave, nor Test's unequalled tide
Reflect his features in their limpid glass.

Unharmed the monarch of the pool shall thrive
In safety 'neath the overhanging bough:
No unsuspected fly will e'er contrive,
(For Marryat is gone!) to reach him now.

I would I had been near him at the last,
To have eased his pain, and held his hand in mine;
They said not he was sick, and so he passed
Into the shadow-land without a sign.

Not more than once to each in life is given,
From such a friend of boyhood's years to part,
My deep regret the chain so sharply riven!
Time, only Time, who smote, can heal the smart.

Surely for him, we may believe, there lies
Some happy hunting ground in realms afar;
Remote from feebler gaze of human eyes,
Some crystal stream beyond the evening star.

Where, due reward for this life's honest work,
The gentle grayling of the almond eye,
And spotted trout by verdant cresses lurk,
And ne'er refuse a well adjusted fly.

There Walton, Francis, aye, and many more,
Those master-minds of intricate device;
Shall meet again on some eternal shore,
To revel in an angler's Paradise.

*Sanctuary added the following note to the poem:
*Eggardon Barrow and Mapperton are both in Dorsetshire: the former
is an old Roman encampment lying close to the famous snipe moor -
Powerstock Common. The latter was Marryat's home in his early days.*

Appendix 1
Last Will and Testament of George Selwyn Marryat

I George Selwyn Marryat residing at number nineteen Hope Terrace Edinburgh with a view to the settlement of my affairs in the event of my death have resolved to execute these presents in manner after written which I hereby declare to be my last will and testament Therefore I do hereby dispose and assign and leave and bequeath to Mrs Lucy Dorothea Marryat my wife in the event of her surviving me the whole property means and estate heritable and moveable real and personal now belonging or which shall belong to me at the time of my death And I do hereby nominate and appoint the said Mrs Lucy Dorothea Marryat and George Edward Eliot Esquire Banker Weymouth and the survivor of them to be my executrix and executor with all the usual powers and I revoke all previous testamentary settlements executed by me and reserve full power to myself to alter or revoke these presents in whole or in part as I shall think proper And I consent to the registration of these presents for preservation In witness whereof these presents written on the face of this sheet of paper by Alexander Cathie Clerk to Messrs Gibson and Strathern writers to the Signet Edinburgh are subscribed by me at Edinburgh the twenty-sixth day of November one thousand and eight hundred and seventy two before these Witnesses John Gibson of number twelve Charlotte Street Edinburgh writer to the Signet and the said Alexander Cathie

> *J Gibson   Witness*
> *Alex Cathie   Witness*   *Geo S Marryat*

Signed by the testator George Selwyn Marryat as his last will and testament in our presence who at the same time in his presence at his request and in the presence of each other have heretofore subscribed our names as witnesses

> *J Gibson of No 12 Charlotte Street   Geo S Marryat*
> *Edinburgh written to the signet*

> *Alex Cathie Clerk to messrs Gibson & Strathern*
> *writer to the signet of No 12 Charlotte Street Edinburgh*

Appendix 2
Extract from the Preface to the Third
(revised) Edition of Dry-Fly Fishing in Theory and Practice,
by F. M. Halford.

In Memoriam George Selwyn Marryat

On the 14th of February, 1896, George Selwyn Marryat died at The Close, Salisbury, aged 56. To his many friends and acquaintances, even to those who had only heard of his skill as a fisherman and his conspicuous unselfishness on the river bank, such an announcement was a source of the deepest regret not unmingled with astonishment that one so young in his ways, so active, strong and vigorous, should have been thus rapidly and suddenly struck down. For fifteen consecutive years we had spent a great proportion of the fishing season together, and scarcely a day passed without my acquiring some knowledge, or learning something new from him. During the close seasons we were frequently staying at one another's houses, and when apart were in daily correspondence on some point connected with the sport, the life history of the insects on which the fish feed, and the best methods of imitating them. Hence it may not be deemed an exaggeration for me to say that his untimely decease was as severe a shock as if I had lost one of my dearest and nearest relations.

'Red Spinner', in an obituary notice in *The Field* of February 22nd, 1896, showed such appreciation of his character and conveyed these impressions in such feeling terms that I am tempted to quote two paragraphs :

'Naturally, with his fame and popularity, he had the run of the choicest streams, but he seldom cared to fill his basket, and I never met an enthusiastic angler - as he was - who so much denied himself the pleasure of fishing at the waterside. But a fish rising in an apparently impossible position would always tempt him, and I have seen him, when an angler had tried his best at a rising fish, and given it over in despair, quietly wait until the said angler had moved out of sight, and then address himself to the rising trout until he had it in the landing net. Wherever Marryat had been fishing, you would always meet someone - keeper, or proprietor, or visiting angler - who before he had been conversing with you for ten minutes about fishing would introduce the name of Marryat as a model for imitation. The days with him by the river were always pleasant and always instructive. If he saw that you really appreciated the knowledge he had obtained, he would take endless trouble to impart it. To the man, however, who fancied himself above everybody else, and who was far above accepting a hint from any living crea-ture, the master was silent, interposing, maybe, a humorous remark sometimes that ought to have made the self-conceited listener feel very small.

'The evenings after the fishing, when dinner being over and the tobacco burning, the discussions turned upon not fishing alone, but a variety of subjects, were, if possible, more delight-ful than the days, for in the course of a busy and, in the early days, adventurous life, Marryat had picked up an astounding mass of information on all manner of topics. Natural history, even abstruser questions of science, he had attacked with the thoroughness which characterised all he did, and there are four or five men still living who probably will never forget a great night at the dear old mill at Houghton, when we led Marryat on to a series of speeches and contentions upon what he called the 'teleology of the infinite'. A more agreeable companion, in short, there never was than George Selwyn Marryat, and it was during those Houghton days that Mr Halford was introduced to him by Francis Francis. This was about the time when Marryat, who was as full of spirits and harmless jokes as a boy, seized the opportunity of Francis being late at breakfast to place empty egg shells, with the unbroken ends upwards, before Francis's plate. Loud was the explosion of laughter when the latter discovered the little trick that had been played upon him. He knew at once who was the author, and with a "What a confounded child you are, Marryat!" joined in the merriment.'

Naturally gifted with a keen sight developed by continual use, possessed of marvellous powers of perception and the faculty of bringing these powers to bear rapidly on any subject, it was not surprising that he should have been full of resource and able without a moment's hesitation to decide how a fish rising in an awkward position should be attacked. At a glance he could see the point from which the cast should be made, and the precise spot where his fly should land to avoid drag. His knowledge of the life history of all common and rare insects, whether bred in the waters or on the land, whether in the larval, pupal, sub-imago, or imago stages, was so great as to render him certain of the class of artificial likely to tempt the fish. His tall, lithe, active figure, a mass of muscle and sinew, enabled him to keep his fly working backwards and forwards in the air. Grasping his rod with a grip like a vice, he put forth all his skill in casting, so as - to use his own expression - to 'combine delicacy and accuracy in the first chuck'. Ready at any time to impart knowledge to a true sportsman, or to find a feeding fish for him, he sacrificed his own chance of sport to crouch at his side, applaud a good attempt, and correct if necessary the faults of an indifferent one, rejoicing more than the tyro himself to see his efforts crowned with success. Full of trite sayings, and brimming over with exuberant spirits like a child, it was '*mens sana in corpore sano*'. Such was the man to whom the first edition of this book was dedicated, and in whose memory this revised one is offered to the angling public.

The probability of a new edition of *Dry-Fly Fishing* being published was often discussed between us, and the late Mr Marryat impressed upon me most strenuously the desirability of making copious notes of errors requiring correction, or amendments tending to keep the general matter thoroughly up to date. This advice was followed, and as lately as January 1895, he carefully read all my notes with the book and sent me a list of a few points which he thought might advantageously be added to them. His words enclosing them were: 'I enclose notes of revise for *Dry-Fly Fishing*. I don't think there is anything else, and I have read it all over again carefully.' After his death, and when the production of this edition was decided, I consulted two of the best dry-fly fishermen of the day, Mr N. Lloyd and Mr W. H. Pope. These good friends each undertook the arduous task of reading through the book and making full notes of any points on which they could suggest improvements on the text of the older editions. My warmest thanks are due to both of them, not only for the time they have devoted to this labour of love, but also for the valuable hints which I have not failed to incorporate in the present work.

April 1st, 1899

To the Fishing Gazette, 28th June, 1884

WHO INVENTED DRY-FLY FISHING?

SIR, I believe the late James Ogden, of Cheltenham, claimed to have been the inventor of the dry-fly system, but I expect it is a case of evolution, and that the first man who threw a dry fly is lost to fame, *caret quia vate sacro*. I see your correspondent, 'Hampshire', saw me cast twenty-eight yards of line with a single-handed rod; it was not measured, and if I were you I should reel in about six yards two feet eleven inches and three-quarters, or you will raise 'Merry Nell' at the forthcoming FISHING GAZETTE Tournament on July 26, unless I come and do it, or burst a little gut trying to do it. I have just been staying at Houghton Mill. I fished one evening at Piddlesworth, and got a brace of fish and two silly dace that hadn't as much judgement as not to rise like grayling, and so met a dry death. I don't hanker after fishing a single blank in hay fields; docks is cusses, and thistles is blasphemy, and all fishermen's recording angels have to be double-balked in hay time. Who might 'Hampshire' be, if it is not a breach of etiquette to say? - I am, &c, . . .

GEO. I. MARRYAT

We must leave 'Hampshire' to make himself known to Mr Marryat, if he cares to do so. We can fully sympathise with Mr Marryat and the exasperating state casting from a hay field induces in all but angels. Last Monday we had a fair dose of this form of hay fever. You see a fish rise just on the edge of the weeds, say within an easy cast upstream, fifteen yards perhaps. You kneel down and creep as near the water as possible to get free of over-hanging green things. Two or three flutters of the fly to dry it, then a nice back cast, and with your eye intent on the feeding place, you make the forward cast. Everything goes nicely until you have got full steam up, and then - bang - your fly has got round a slender but tough bit of rye grass, or the red scale-like flowers of the dock. On such an occasion the best thing to do is to set your teeth well into the screw of your whisky flask and take a solar observation, remember the 'World's' advice as to what to say, and repeat 'Godfrey Daniel's blast and furnace works' until relieved. Repeat it to the farmer if he asks you why you don't walk 'all over the field'. - ED.

To The Field, 8th January, 1881

QUILL BODIES FOR FLIES

It may be advisable, for the benefit of the enthusiasts in fly fishing who still tie their own flies, to give a few hints on the materials mentioned by Mr Francis, in his charming article in the Christmas number of *The Field*, as 'quill'. Let no one suppose for a minute that he can get it from his 'grey goose quill', or any ordinary feather. It requires careful selection and careful dyeing to arrive at a satisfactory result. It is obtained from the tail feather of the peacock; a single *herl* is divested of the metallic fur which adheres to it by repeatedly drawing the strand sharply downwards, from the point to the heel, between the ball of the forefinger and the thumb nail of the right hand, the end of the strand being held in the left hand. The strands from the eye of the peacock's feather are those selected; those from below the eye of the feather will be found to be of a uniform dark dun, and are of little use, as they are too dark to take the light-olive or brown tints required for the bodies of the duns and spinners, for which alone they are useful. The strands from the eye of the feather are of a lighter dun (if obtained from a good feather, those with the largest eyes being the best), having one edge of much lighter colour than the other. It is this that gives the ribbed appearance to the body of the fly when tied, which constitutes it killing quality. I remember a fisherman on the Itchen telling me one day that he had killed with a partic-ular quill gnat which he showed me, having this rib, while he could not do anything with any of the rest of the half-dozen which he had bought with it though they were otherwise exactly the same in hackle and wing. But to return to our quill. Having, as I said, selected a good feather, cut off the eye about half and inch below the metallic green; the rest is valueless for quill bodies. If, on stripping a strand, it shows nearly all the width a pale colour, you are right; if not, go higher up the eye. For grey quill gnat the natural colour is right, and with a light blue dun hackle, and light starling wing, it is a deadly fly on a bright day; the same with darker wing and hackle is better for a cloudy day. The quill dyed olive with onion dye, and a blue dun hackle dyed in the same dye is three shades and sizes, no fisherman should ever be without. I should not be afraid to back it against any other single fly that can be tied. For the brown dun mentioned by Mr Francis I use Judson's olive-brown, which looks purple when mixed with water, but, *mirabile dictu!* dyes olive-brown. This, with a ginger-brown hackle, and starling (or, for a change, coot) wing, is a nailer for the autumn moths. A fine red spinner is tied by using Judson's light red for the quill, with a coch-y-bonddu hackle and light dun wings. This fly should be ribbed with very fine gold wire. Of course, these flies may be varied to any extent by dyeing to match any required shade. If a fly is required of a uniform colour, the quill should be so laid on that the light edge of the quill overlaps and hides the dark edge. This lightens the colour of the fly considerably, but does away with the ribbed look of the body. I think white peacock herl would make a good dyed body, but have been hitherto unable to procure any, though I have been promised some by several friends. The roots of some of the strands of the longest tail feathers of the peacock are sometimes nearly white for an inch or two from the base. I have used them for light/brown/duns with success. For all the dyes the feather should be soaked in hot alum mordant before attempting to dye them, and they should be well washed in cold water when the tint required is obtained, or the quill will rot. I do not agree with the theory of Ronald, that a fish spits out a hard-bodied fly of quill or hair quicker than a soft-bodied one of fur or dubbing. Anyway, if he does, it is good enough for me if I can get him to take it into his mouth at all; and that takes some doing on parts of the Itchen and Test nowadays.

G.T.M (*sic*)

Our correspondent is a past master in the art, as may be easily seen and all his advice may be relied on. Can any correspondent oblige us with the eyes of a few tail feathers from a white peacock? - ED.

Bibliography

The main printed sources of reference are as follows. References were also made to articles published on the Internet and in magazines, and material held by the National Archives.

Beazley, David, 'The Saga of the "Snecky-Limerick" ', *The Flyfishers*, Summer 1995, Volume 84, No. 299, and Winter 1995, Volume 84, No. 300, The Flyfishers' Club, London

Fisher, Major A. T., *Rod and River or Fly-Fishing for Salmon, Trout and Grayling*, Richard Bentley and Son, London, 1892

Francis, Francis, *A Book on Angling*, Longmans, Green, And Co, London, 1885
Angling Reminiscences. , Horace Cox, London, 1887

Freeman, Michael, *Railways and the Victorian Imagination*, Yale University Press, New Haven and London, 1999

Glasspool, Jim, (Editor), *The Test and Itchen Association Ltd, Millenium Report*, The Test and Itchen Association Ltd, Hampshire, 2000

Grey, Viscount of Fallodon, *Fly Fishing*, J. M. Dent & Sons Ltd, London, 1931

Griffiths, Terry, 'The "Portmanteau" of George Selwyn Marryat', *The Flyfishers*, Summer 2009, The Flyfishers' Club, London

Haggard, H. Rider, *Rural England Vol I*, Longmans, Green, And Co, London, 1906

Halford, F. M., 'The Hundred Best Patterns of Floating Flies', *Baily's Magazine of Sports and Pastimes*, London, 1896
'Twenty-one Years of a Chalk-Stream Diary', *Baily's Magazine of Sports and Pastimes*, London, 1899
An Angler's Autobiography, Vinton & Co., Limited, London, 1903
The Dry-Fly Man's Handbook, George Routledge & Sons, Limited, London, 1913
Dry-Fly Fishing, Theory and Practice, Barry Shurlock, Reading, 1973
Floating Flies and how to dress them, Barry Shurlock, Winchester, 1974
Modern Development of the Dry Fly, The Flyfishers' Classic Library, Moretonhampstead, 2005

Hall, H. S., 'A Bird Famous in the Annals of Fly Dressing', *The Field*, 19 March, 1910, London

Hart, Col. H. G., *The New Annual Army List, and Militia List* (various years), John Murray, London

Hawker, Peter, *The Diary of Colonel Peter Hawker*, 1802-1853, Vol II, Greenhill Books, London, 1988

Hayter, Tony, 'Dr Thomas Sanctuary, 1852-1931', *The Flyfishers*, Summer 2003, London
F.M. Halford and the Dry-Fly Revolution, Robert Hale Limited, London, 2002

Herd, Andrew, *The Fly*, The Medlar Press Limited, Ellesmere, 2003

Hills, John Waller, *River Keeper, The Life of William James Lunn*, Geoffrey Bles, London, 1934

Holmes, Richard, *Sahib, The British Soldier in India*, 1750-1914, Harper Collins Publishers, London, 2005

Keen, Joseph, *Fluorescent Flies*, Herbert Jenkins Limited, London, 1964

Lapsley, Peter, 'I Wish I'd Fished with - George Selwyn Marryat', *Fly-Fishers' Journal*, Winter 2002, Volume 87, No 314

Lawrie, W. H., *All-Fur Flies & How to Dress Them*, Pelham Books Ltd, London, 1967

Lloyd, Christopher, *Captain Marryat and the Old Navy*, Longmans, Green and Co, Ltd, London,1939

Macintyre, Stuart, *A Concise History of Australia*, Cambridge University Press, Cambridge, 1999

Marinaro, Vincent, *A Modern Dry-Fly Code*, The Flyfisher's Classic Library, Bovey Tracey, 1996

Martin, Darrell, *The Fly-Fisher's Craft*, The Art and History, The Lyons Press, Connecticut, 2006

Maxwell, Sir Herbert (Editor), *Chronicles of The Houghton Fishing Club*, 1822-1908, Edward Arnold, London, 1908

McDonald, John (Editor), *The Complete Fly Fisherman, The Notes*

and Letters of Theodore Gordon, Jonathan Cape, London, 1949

Mingay, G.E. (Editor), *The Victorian Countryside*, Vol I, Routledge & Keegan Paul, London, 1981

Morgan, John, 'George Selwyn Marryat - his Portmanteau', *The Flyfishers*, Summer 2004 and Winter 2004, The Flyfishers' Club, London

Newman, John and Nikolaus, *The Buildings of England, Dorset*, Penguin Books, London, Pevsner, 1993

Orwin, Christabel S. & Whetham, Edith H., *History of British Agriculture 1846-1914*, David & Charles, Newton Abbot, 1971

Pain, C. Ernest, *Fifty Years on The Test*, Philip Allan, London, 1934

Pocock, Tom, *Captain Marryat, Seaman, Writer and Adventurer*, Chatham Publishing, London, 2000

Ransome, Arthur, *Rod and Line*, Oxford University Press, Oxford, 1980

Ritchie, Jack, *The Australian Trout, Its Introduction and Acclimatisation in Victorian Waters*, The Victorian Fly-Fisher's Association, Melbourne, 1988

Robson, Kenneth, (Editor), *The Essential G. E. M. Skues*, A & C Black, London, 1998

Russell, Harold, *Chalkstream and Moorland, Thoughts on Trout-Fishing*, Smith, Elder & Co., London, 1911

Senior, William, *Travel and Trout in The Antipodes*, Chatto and Windus, London, 1880

Near and Far, An Angler's Sketches of Home Sport and Colonial Life, Sampson Low, Marston, Searle, and Rivington, London, 1888

Lines in Pleasant Places, Being the Aftermath of an Old Angler, Simpkin, Marshall, Hamilton, Kent & Co. Ltd., London, 1920

Skues, G. E. M., Grey, *Journal of the Fly-Fishers' Club*, Autumn 1933 Volume 22, No 87,

The Way Of A Trout With A Fly, And Some Further Studies in Minor Tactics, A & C Black, London, 1949

The Chalk-Stream Angler, Sidelines, Sidelights and Reflections, Barry Shurlock & Co, Winchester, 1976

Nymph Fishing For Chalk Stream Trout combined with Minor Tactics of The Chalk Stream, A&C Black, London, 1979

Itchen Memories, Robert Hale, London, 1999

Smythe, The Very Rev. P. M., *The Diary of an All-Round Angler*, Faber and Faber Limited, London, 1956

Sweeney, Christopher, *Transported: In place of Death*, The Macmillan Company of Australia Pty Ltd, 1981

Thomas, David St John & Whitehouse, Patrick, *The Great Days of the Country Railway*, David & Charles, Newton Abbot, 2002

Thompson, F. M. L., *English Landed Society in the Nineteenth Century*, Routledge & Keegan Paul, London, 1963

Vines, Sidney, *The English Chalk Streams*, B. T. Batsford Ltd, London 1992

Wade, Henry, *Rod-Fishing in Clear Waters*, by Fly, Minnow, and Worm, Bell and Daldy, London, 1860

Walbran, Francis M., *Grayling And How To Catch Them and Recollections Of A Sportsman*, The Flyfishers' Classic Library, Moretonhampstead, 2004

Walker, C. F. (Editor), *The Complete Fly-Fisher*, Herbert Jenkins Ltd, London, 1963

Warner, Oliver, *Captain Marryat, A Rediscovery*, Constable and Company Ltd, London, 1953

Warner, Philip, *The British Cavalry*, J. M. Dent & Sons Ltd, London, 1984

Wiggin, Maurice, (Editor), *The Angler's Bedside Book*, BT Batsford, London, 1965

Index